PROPHET FOR THE FINAL GENERATION

Studies on the Theological and Interpretative
Authority of the Gift of Prophecy

Editor: Allan Bornape
Cover design: Catalina Reyes
Cover image: Charles Fitch (1842)
Inside design: Luz Helena Robledo

Printed in the United States
First edition: 2024
ISBN: 978-1-962113-02-1

Aditional copies of this book in English or Spanish
are available in our Websites:
arrowofsalvation.org

Saeta de Salvacion (dba Arrow of Salvation) is a legally registered non-profit
organization, recognized as a 501(c)3 entity, dedicated to preserving, and multiplying
the end-time Present Truth message entrusted by God to the Seventh-day Adventist
Church to proclaim to the world. We are a supporting ministry of the Seventh-day
Adventist Church and actively participate as a member of the ASI and the OCI.

Contents

Foreword

One of the most striking and moving events in the Holy Scriptures is the divine judgment against King David by the prophet Nathan (2 Sam. 12:1-24). By means of a parable, the prophet provoked David to acknowledge his flagrant sin, and in the act, to condemn himself against himself. However, after the king's acknowledgment ("I sinned against the Lord," 2 Sam. 12:13), and his deep repentance recorded in Psalm 51, God spared his life, but the consequences of his sin brought war forever upon his house, along with the death of his first-born with Bathsheba. David, statesman, musician, warrior and poet, who became the greatest king in the history of Israel, had to be exhorted by heaven through a prophet of the Lord. God decided not to send a priest, a leader of Israel or a prince. He sent a prophet.

What would have happened if the king had not repented, if he had rejected the prophetic call? The whole history of Israel would have been shaken, from the monarchy, the temple (built by his son), and, above all, the sacred lineage through which the Messiah would come: "I am the root and the offspring of David, the bright and morning star" (Rev. 22:16b). For the last days of history, God also raised up a prophet to exhort his people and guide them to the second coming of Christ. This is the portrait of the book of Revelation, where the remnant appears alongside the prophetic gift (Rev. 12:17; 14:12; 19:10). For the last generation of the faithful, the prophetic gift is the indispensable divine resource for their existence and purpose in the world. To reject this gift or to neglect it would be an enormous mistake with grave consequences.

Pastor Gerard Damsteegt's book is a work that offers us a profound reflection on some of the fundamental aspects of the prophetic gift as manifested in the person of Ellen White. It brings together four previously published articles, where the author analyzes the themes of the inspiration of the Scriptures, the lifestyle, the interpretation of the Bible and the place of Adventist theologians in their relationship with the use of the Testimonies.

What is particularly relevant in this book is that Pastor Damsteegt writes, in great detail, about each subject according to the view that Ellen White developed, that is, from the vision that a prophet has about the mentioned subjects. With the precision of a noted historian and the rigor of a scholar with more than 40 years of experience, the book discusses the serious hermeneutical problems that Adventism (and Christianity in general) faces today, the power contained in a healthy diet and life habits, and its close link with the sanctity of life (cf. Dan. 1:8; Lev. 11:44-45), or how a correct understanding of the inspiration of the Bible prevents us from false theories and harmful teachings.

The last chapter of the book stands out, with a lucid reflection on the connection of the theologians of the church with the three angels' messages, where the author warns of the crucial role of the gift of prophecy for a correct interpretation of the solemn messages and their application for the fulfillment of the mission of the church.

The book you hold in your hands is a valuable text that can provide a renewed appreciation of the Testimonies of the Spirit of Prophecy, its special theological authority for the end times, and, in short, for a solid and clear interpretation of the truths of salvation that God desires for His church. For "He revealeth the deep and hidden things: he knoweth the things which are in darkness, and with him dwelleth light" (Dan. 2:22). And we are told that the Lord's method of choice was this: "For the Lord GOD will do nothing, except he reveal his secret to his servants the prophets" (Amos 3:7).

The Editors

1

Inspiration of the Scriptures in the Writings of Ellen G. White

Recently the subject of inspiration has received increased attention among Seventh-day Adventists. A growing number of believers are beginning to realize that one's view of the inspiration of the Bible has far reaching implications for one's daily decisions and lifestyle.

All Seventh-day Adventists believe the Biblical teaching on the Sabbath and what happens when one dies. All believe that they have a special mission in calling people to the true worship of God. All believe that the body is the temple of God. All believe women should serve God.

But beyond the general themes there is not as much consensus. It is here that the specific view of the inspiration of the Bible makes a significant difference in how its directives are applied to the life. When confronted with the biblical text that addresses specifics not many Seventh-day Adventists would say, "I don't believe what Scripture says there!"

Instead, there is a reason, a context, a cultural/or "for those times" consideration cited. It is not so much that there is a base disbelief in Scripture, but an interpretive difference at the root of all Christian controversy. It is precisely here where deep hermeneutical differences divide all Christian groups. As some Seventh-day Adventists seem increasingly uncertain about which hermeneutical tools are appropriate, there is the potential for an ever-increasing number of tensions

Originally published in the Journal of the Adventist Theological Society, 5/1 (1994):155-179. Used with permission.

and conflicts among us. Fundamental to all schism is the question of inspiration, the age- old: "How Readest Thou?"

Ellen White, largely regarded by Adventists as a prophetess, has provided important insights on the value and interpretation of Scripture throughout her life. In this article I investigate Ellen White's views of inspiration. She had very definite ideas on the inspiration of the Bible and its implications for everyday living. My research has analyzed all her references to inspiration as retrieved by a CD-ROM from all her published works.

I will deal with questions like "What is the relationship between the Bible and inspiration?" "What is the nature of inspiration?" "How does Biblical inspiration function?" "What are the unique characteristics of inspiration?" "What are its functions?" "What are the evidences of Biblical inspiration?" "How does doubt effect one's view of inspiration?" "What are erroneous views and attitudes on inspiration, and how should we study the subject of inspiration?"

The Bible and Inspiration

The inspiration of human beings by God made the Bible what God intended it to be—His unique Word. Towards the end of her life, commenting on the efficacy of Scripture, Ellen White calls the inspiration of the Word: God's great work . Says she, God "does not design to add a new element of efficiency to his Word; He has done His great work in giving His inspiration to the Word."[1]

Throughout her life she saw an intimate relation between the Bible and inspiration. She equates the Bible with "inspiration,"[2] the "Word of inspiration,"[3] "words of inspiration,"[4] the "volume of inspi-

1   "Accepted in the Beloved," *Review and Herald,* October 15, 1908, 7.
2   *The Faith I Live By,* 116.
3   *Manuscript Releases,* 1:52.
4   *Gospel Workers,* (1892), 123. See also *Fundamentals of Christian Education,* 351 on students' health and inspiration.

ration,"[5] the "testimony of inspiration,"[6] the "great treasure house of inspired truth,"[7] and the "test of all inspiration."[8]

We will now investigate her views on the nature of inspiration.

The Nature of Inspiration

What is the nature of inspiration? How does it affect different people and what is the process by which it operates? Seventh-day Adventists believe that the Bible writers were inspired when they wrote. Consequently, they reject the idea of degrees of inspiration which implies that some parts of Scripture are less inspired than others. They hold that the whole Bible is fully inspired. In this they have accepted the position that Ellen White took in opposition to the theory of degrees of inspiration when it was introduced among Adventists in the 1880's.

However, Ellen White makes a distinction between biblical prophets who spoke by "direct inspiration" and teachers in the schools of the prophets who were not directly inspired. She comments: "In the highest sense the prophet was one who spoke by direct inspiration, communicating to the people the messages he had received from God. But the name [prophet] was given also to those who, though not so directly inspired, were divinely called to instruct the people in the works and ways of God. For the training of such a class of teachers, Samuel, by the Lord's direction, established the schools of the prophets."[9]

Bible writers who spoke by "direct inspiration" are inspired in the "fullest sense of the word." When asked whether the Adventist pioneers were inspired by God, she answered, "I dare not say they were not led of God, for Christ leads into all truth; but when it comes to inspiration in the fullest sense of the word, I answer, No."[10]

---

5   *Patriarchs and Prophets*, 596.

6   *Great Controversy*, 341; *Spirit of Prophecy*, 4:211.

7   *Great Controversy*, 193; *Spirit of Prophecy*, 4:152.

8   Ibid.

9   *Education*, 46.

10   "Open the Heart to Light," *Review and Herald*, March 25, 1890, 177; *Counsels to Writers and Editors*, 34; *Evangelism*, 297.

Today, Bible students frequently classify these two groups under the categories of inspiration and illumination. Following this arrangement, Bible writers fall under the category of inspiration, all others under illumination. Ellen White does not use this terminology but employs "inspiration" and "illumination" as synonyms.[11] In most cases when she applies the word "illumination" to Bible writers, she describes them not simply as having "illumination" but "special illumination."[12]

Since our concern is with the nature of biblical inspiration, we move now to address these questions: How did Ellen White view inspiration as it worked in the divinely qualified writers of Scripture?

The Process of Biblical Inspiration. Ellen White describes the inspiration of the Bible as a process by which the utterances of humans become the word of God. Key elements in this process are God's inspiration of all Scripture, the incarnation of the Word, the role of the Holy Spirit and the transformation of human words into the Word of God.

All Scripture is given by inspiration of God. Ellen White frequently asserts that the Scriptures are "given by inspiration of God". She writes: "The Bible points to God as its author; yet it was written by human hands; and in the varied style of its different books it presents the characteristics of the several writers. The truths revealed are all 'given by inspiration of God' (2 Tim 3:16); yet they are expressed in the words of men."[13]

In contrast to common practice today, she avoids calling the writers of the various Bible books "authors." Her focus remains on God as the sole Author of the Scriptures while the humans involved without exception are described as writers, not authors. This is fully in harmony with her general purpose to present the Bible as the inspired Word of God.

---

11 See e.g. *Desire of Ages*, 464.
12 *Great Controversy*, 344; *Acts of the Apostles*, 452.
13 *Great Controversy*, v; *The Faith I Live By*, 10; *Selected Messages* 1:25.

The Word was made flesh. Ellen White perceives from the incarnate nature of Christ, ("the Word was made flesh," John 1:14) far-reaching theological implications for the written Word. She reasons that, as Christ's nature is made up of a union of the divine and the human, so also is the nature of the Bible. The rationale for this divine-human nature is God's attempt to adapt the Word of God to human needs. The following comment succinctly expresses her view:

The union of the divine and the human, manifest in Christ, exists also in the Bible. The truths revealed are all "given by inspiration of God;" yet they are expressed in the words of men and are adapted to human needs. Thus it may be said of the Book of God, as it was of Christ, that "the Word was made flesh, and dwelt among us." And this fact, so far from being an argument against the Bible, should strengthen faith in it as the word of God."[14]

This is why she can describe the Bible as the embodiment of divine thought in "human language."[15]

What impact did this divine–human union have on the language of the Bible? Was it written in superhuman language? Ellen White denies this, because "the Bible was written for practical purposes." She explains: "Jesus, in order to reach man where he is, took humanity. The Bible must be given in the language of men. Everything that is human is imperfect. Different meanings are expressed by the same word; there is not one word for each distinct idea."[16]

Is the language of Scripture God's mode of thought and expression? Again Ellen White would answer "No." Its language is "that of humanity. God, as a writer, is not represented. Men will often say such an expression is not like God. But God has not put Himself in words, in logic, in rhetoric, on trial in the Bible. The writers of the Bible were God's penmen, not His pen."[17]

---

14   *Testimonies for the Church,* 5:747.
15   *Selected Messages,* 1:25.
16   Ibid., 1:20.
17   Ibid., 1:21. She also writes: "The Lord speaks to human beings in imperfect speech, in

In spite of the limitations and the imperfections of the human writers and language, God accomplished His purpose. "The Lord," she remarks, "gave His word in just the way He wanted it to come." Using an illustration from nature, she says, "There is variety in a tree, there are scarcely two leaves just alike. Yet this variety adds to the perfection of the tree as a whole."[18]

The role of the Holy Spirit. The process of inspiration involves the Godhead and especially the Holy Spirit. In describing the inspiration of Bible writers Ellen White states, "They were moved by the Holy Spirit" (2 Peter 1:21). She does not limit this moving by the Spirit solely to the giving of prophecy as has been suggested recently,[19] but applies it to the impartation of the whole Bible. She writes, "The Bible was written by men who were moved by the Holy Ghost."[20] "The Infinite One by his Holy Spirit has shed light into the minds and hearts of his servants. He has given dreams and visions, symbols and figures."[21]

Angels of God are closely associated with the Holy Spirit in the process of inspiration. Their function is to shed light on the person who is under inspiration.[22]

The role of the Spirit in inspiring the Bible writers can be described as follows: He is responsible for communicating specific mes-

---

order that the degenerate senses, the dull, earthly perception, of earthly beings may comprehend His words. Thus is shown God's condescension. He meets fallen human beings where they are. The Bible, perfect as it is in its simplicity, does not answer to the great ideas of God; for infinite ideas cannot be perfectly embodied in finite vehicles of thought. Instead of the expressions of the Bible being exaggerated, as many people suppose, the strong expressions break down before the magnificence of the thought, though the penman selected the most expressive language through which to convey the truths of higher education. Sinful beings can only bear to look upon a shadow to the brightness of heaven's glory. Ibid., 1:22.

18 Ibid., 1:21.

19 See George E. Rice, *Luke, a Plagiarist?* (Mountain View, CA: Pacific Press Publ. Assn., 1983).

20 "Obedience the Fruit of Union with Christ—No. 1," *Review and Herald,* August 27, 1901, 551. See also *SDA Bible Commentary,* 7:945; *Selected Messages,* 1:19, 20; "Christ Revealed the Father," *Review and Herald,* January 7, 1890, 1; "The Parable of the Sower,"*Bible Echo and Signs of the Times,* August 19, 1895, 239. The Bible, she says, "is the inspiration of One infallible, the divine communication to holy men of old, who spoke as they were moved by the Holy Ghost." "The Parable of the Sower," *Review and Herald* 10-03-99/07.

21 *Great Controversy,* v; *The Faith I Live By,* 10; *Selected Messages,* 1:25.

22 *Patriarchs and Prophets,* 251.

sages to the writers as well as how they are to express it. In this process His purpose is to so hide the writer in Christ that he recedes into the background and God and His message are exalted. Says she: "The Holy Spirit has so shaped matters, both in the giving of the prophecy, and in the events portrayed, as to teach that the human agent is to be kept out of sight, hid in Christ, and the Lord God of heaven and His law are to be exalted."[23]

In communicating truth there is a fine balance between the actions of the Holy Spirit and human freedom. Ellen White says, the Holy Spirit expresses truth "according to the development" of the writer's mind but without the mind being "cramped, as if forced into a certain mold."[24]

Human words transformed into the Word of God. Although it is abundantly clear that Ellen White considers the Bible the inspired Word of God, she points out that it is "not the words of the Bible that are inspired, but the men that were inspired." "Inspiration," she says, "acts not on the man's words or his expressions but on the man himself, who, under the influence of the Holy Ghost, is imbued with thoughts. But the words receive the impress of the individual mind." The end product is amazing: "The divine mind is diffused. The divine mind and will is combined with the human mind and will; thus the utterances of the man are the word of God."[25] Thus human words become God's Word.

Lifestyle and Inspiration. What kind of persons were directly inspired? What was their lifestyle? How perfect were they?

Bible characters were not infallible. Throughout the Scripture the uniform testimony is that its writers were not infallible persons. They had weaknesses inherent with fallen human nature. For example, Peter revealed a hypocritical attitude for which Paul strongly rebuked him (Gal 2:11, 12). In another instance James gave Paul the unfortunate advice that was largely responsible for bringing about Paul's first Roman imprisonment (Acts 21:20- 26).[26] David committed adultery

---

23   *Evangelism,* 577.
24   *Selected Messages,* 1:22.
25   Ibid., 1:21.
26   *Sketches from the Life of Paul,* 214; *Bible Commentary,* 6:1065.

and murder, and God would not even allow him to build His temple. Solomon had his years of blatant backsliding. Yet these were Bible writers. But because their opinions and lifestyle proved at times to be biased or immoral should their writings be disqualified?

What were the circumstances under which they sometimes erred or sinned? It is possible that their failures occurred when they were not under the direct influence of the Spirit's inspiration.

Inspiration guarantees trustworthy Scripture. A very natural question is: How human beings, who by nature are fallible, could possibly speak or write things that would be considered the infallible word of God? One might address this question in another way: Are there circumstances under which fallible Bible characters could speak or write truth without error? Ellen White replies with a resounding "Yes"!

The circumstance under which a Bible writer could present messages without error was when he was under the direct influence of the Spirit of the Lord. When the otherwise fallible Jacob came to the end of his life, he prophesied under "the spirit of inspiration." The result was, Ellen White says, that he disclosed with amazing accuracy before his sons "their past life, and their future history, revealing the purposes of God in regard to them."[27]

It is, therefore, clear that Bible writers themselves were not infallible but subject to the inherent weaknesses of their fallen human nature. Yet when under the direct inspiration of the Holy Spirit, they presented a message that was fully trustworthy and without error.

The Importance of Understanding Inspiration

As discussed earlier, the day to day decisions most believers make on the basis of the Bible depends, to a great extent, on their view of inspiration and more particular on their ability or failure to understand inspiration's unique characteristics and function. We will first focus on Ellen White's views of the characteristics of inspiration, then its function.

---

27   *Spiritual Gifts*, 3:170. Other examples are Balaam, David and Solomon.

Characteristics of Biblical Inspiration

What are the specific characteristics of "direct inspiration"? What is the effect of inspiration on the Bible? How does it affect the Bible's accuracy and trustworthiness? How does inspiration communicate God's voice?

It is accurate and fully trustworthy. To what extent can the Bible be trusted? Is it accurate? Did the writers make mistakes or errors? These are questions that occupy the minds of many. The measure of assurance they have about these questions determines some people's ability to believe in God; some have rejected Christianity altogether over such issues. Beyond basic belief, a person's commitment to following specific counsels and requirements of Scriptures is affected by his/her perception of trustworthiness. We could say that believers' confidence in God is in direct proportion to their confidence in the trustworthiness of the Bible.

Ellen White gives resounding assurance that the Scriptures can be fully trusted. Her message is clear: The Bible is the infallible Word of God. She wholeheartedly endorses "the grand principle" held by the Waldenses, Wycliffe, Huss, Luther, Zwingli, and other reformers on "the infallible authority of the Holy Scriptures as a rule of faith and practice."[28]

In response to the question about the possibility of mistakes by copyists or translators, she says: "This is all probable, and the mind that is so narrow that it will hesitate and stumble over this possibility or probability would be just as ready to stumble over the mysteries of the Inspired Word, because their feeble minds cannot see through the purposes of God." "Yes," she adds, "they would just as easily stumble over plain facts that the common mind will accept." She assures believers that "all the mistakes will not cause trouble to one soul, or cause any feet to stumble, that would not manufacture difficulties from the plainest revealed truth."[29]

Ellen White points out that in the transmission of the text, attempts were made at times to improve the text, but these changes were not

---

28 *Great Controversy*, 249. See also Ibid. 68, 102, 143, 173, 177, 238.
29 *Selected Messages*, 1:16.

for the better: "When copies of it [Bible] were few, learned men had in some instances changed the words, thinking that they were making it more plain, when in reality they were mystifying that which was plain, by causing it to lean to their established views, which were governed by tradition."[30] In her remarks Ellen White does not clearly state that the Bible contains mistakes, she only refers to the "possibility or probability" of mistakes through copying and translating, and indicates that in some cases the obvious meaning of the text through changes has become more difficult to understand. Never, however, in her writings does she make the slightest allusion to the idea that the Bible writers themselves made mistakes.

In assuring the total trustworthiness of the biblical record, Ellen White affirms that it is a product of "the unerring pen of inspiration."[31] Consequently "it never makes a mistake."[32] The Bible "is infallible," she says, "for God cannot err."[33] Believers, therefore, can be fully confident that "in the Bible we have the unerring counsel of God."[34]

At a time when more and more people feel that everything they read is biased and that objectivity is impossible, it is refreshing to know that an accurate and unbiased source of information is available in the Bible.

Often biographies of Christians portray practically faultless characters. Such shine as examples of immaculate piety and fail to reveal that these are, in fact, erring human beings subject to our common temptations. The inherent weakness of these biographies or autobiographies is that "it is next to a human impossibility to lay open our faults for the possible inspection of our friends."[35] Minds "are so subject to prejudice that it is not possible for human histories to be absolutely impartial."[36] Thus such histories always reveal human biases.

---

30   *Early Writings*, 220-221.
31   "Jacob and Esau," *Signs of the Times*, April 17, 1879, 122.
32   *The Kress Collection*, 98.
33   *My Life Today*, 27.
34   *Testimonies*, 4:441. See also *Messages to Young People*, 443.
35   "Bible Biographies," *Review and Herald*, January 22, 1880, 49.
36   *Patriarchs and Prophets*, 238.

By contrast, Ellen White assures us that the histories in the Bible have the unique quality of being "absolutely impartial." She writes that through inspiration we have a faithful record of "the faults of good men, those who were distinguished by the favor of God; indeed, their faults are more fully presented than their virtues." How did the inspired writers obtain these accurate historical records? Says she, "The scribes of God wrote as they were dictated by the Holy Spirit, having no control of the work themselves."[37] No wonder that she could write that in the Bible "only can we find a history of our race unsullied by human prejudice or human pride."[38]

"One of the best evidences of the authority of the Scriptures," Ellen White says, is that "the truth is not glossed over, nor the sins of its chief characters suppressed."[39] She adds that "had the Bible been written by uninspired persons, it would no doubt have presented the character of its honored men in a more flattering light. But as it is, we have a correct record of their experiences."[40]

The question inevitably arises, How is it humanly possible to be absolutely impartial? It is here where the unique character of inspiration plays such a crucial role. She points out that through divine inspiration the Bible writer, "lifted above the weaknesses of humanity, tells the simple, naked truth."[41] From a human perspective it is impossible to reach this level of precision. It is only those who experience divine inspiration in the "fullest sense of the word"[42] who are able to produce unbiased, unerring accounts. It is this quality of reporting under the full control of the Holy Spirit that validates the Scriptures.

Divine inspiration forms the basis for the assuring promise: "the Word of God is given as a lamp unto our feet, and a light unto our path" (Ps 119:105). Ellen White cites its relevance for discovering prehistoric mysteries as well as the future. "Inspiration," she states, "in giving us the history of the Flood, has explained wonderful mys-

---

37 *Testimonies* 4:9. She also comments that the writings of the apostles were "dictated by the Holy Ghost" (*Spiritual Gifts* 1:176).
38 *Patriarchs and Prophets*, 596.
39 Ibid., 4:9; *Patriarchs and Prophets*, 238.
40 *Patriarchs and Prophets*, 238.
41 "Bible Biographies," *Review and Herald*, January 22, 1880, 49.
42 *Ellen G. White 1888 Materials*, 547; *Counsels to Writers and Editors*, 34.

teries, that geology, independent of inspiration, never could."[43] At the same time Bible prophecy accurately portrays the future, often in great detail.[44]

Inspiration is one key that leads to the discovery of harmony between science and the Bible. Science, independent of God, she says is "pretentious ignorance" which has a "deceptive power "that "has captivated and enslaved the minds of many." But "true science and inspiration are in perfect harmony."[45]

Her personal testimony on the absolute trustworthiness of the Bible is simple and straightforward: "I take the Bible just as it is, as the Inspired Word. I believe its utterances in an entire Bible."[46] "The Word of God is infallible, accept it as it reads."[47]

It is God's voice speaking to the soul. The testimony of inspired writings has the unique characteristic of being the voice of God. This quality makes Scripture of vital importance for believers who desire to discover God's will for their lives. "Search the Scriptures," she says, "for therein is the counsel of God, the voice of God speaking to the soul."[48] Daily we need to learn "from the word of God, which is the man of our counsel."[49] Through the Bible God leads us to our full potential. "The word of God is like a treasure house, containing everything that is essential to perfect the man of God."[50]

Inspired Scripture provides a sufficient rule of faith and practice under all circumstances. "The teaching of this Word is exactly that needed in all circumstances in which we may be placed. It is a sufficient rule of faith and practice; for it is the voice of God speaking to the soul, giving the members of his family directions for keeping the heart with all diligence."[51]

---

43 *Lift Him Up,* 59. See also *Spirit of Prophecy,* 1:89; *Spiritual Gifts,* 3:94.
44 *Spirit of Prophecy,* 3:156, 160.
45 *Testimonies,* 4:584. See also *Messages to Young People,* 190.
46 *Selected Messages,* 1:17.
47 "The Tasmanian Campmeeting," *Review and Herald,* February 11, 1896, 81.
48 *Fundamentals of Christian Education,* 391. See *Kress Collection* 98.
49 *Kress Collection,* 98.
50 *Fundamentals of Christian Education,* 123. *In Heavenly Places,* 133.
51 "The Word of God," *Review and Herald,* August 22, 1907, 8. She says, "The Bible is an infallible guide under all circumstances," *My Life Today,* 25.

Consequently Scripture, being the voice of God, is the best source of counsel. Instead of depending on church leadership to settle minor and major matters, she encourages believers to carry these things to God. "The Lord can be approached by all" she says. "He is much more accessible than the president of the General Conference." "Lead these men who have ability and talent to look to God, that they may be taught by Him. Teach them to go to the Fountainhead for instruction in righteousness." Because "all Scripture is given by inspiration of God," she asks, "What then, is your excuse for turning for counsel from One who is infinite in wisdom to finite men, who are as weak as yourselves? One has suffered for you, the Just for the unjust."[52]

It presents the Bible as a self-interpreting book. Inspiration sets Scripture apart from other books, making it a category by itself and containing its own principles of interpretation. "The Bible is its own expositor," Ellen White explains. "One passage will prove to be a key that will unlock other passages, and in this way light will be shed upon the hidden meaning of the word. By comparing different texts treating on the same subject, viewing their bearing on every side, the true meaning of the Scriptures will be made evident."[53]

This important characteristic of inspiration has made the Bible a book that the uneducated can comprehend as well as the educated. Ellen White writes: "The words of inspiration are so plain that the unlearned may understand them."[54] "Take the Bible as your study-book. All can understand its instruction."[55]

Functions of Inspiration

Inspiration has several vital functions to perform that are indispensable for believers who are preparing for the return of the Lord. These functions can be grouped into five categories: Revealing God's character, perfecting the character of His people, making every Bible

---

52 *Testimonies to Ministers*, 329-330.
53 "The Science of Salvation The First of Sciences," *Review and Herald*, December 1, 1891, 737.
54 *Gospel Workers*, (1892), 123.
55 *Gospel Workers*, (1915), 309.

passage profitable, pointing out human limitations and providing a foundation for Christian education.

To reveal God's character. An important purpose of inspiration is to reveal God. Ellen White points out that God has revealed Himself in two ways: "Through the volume of inspiration"—the Scriptures—and through "the book of nature "which is shown in the "works of creation."[56] It is in the Bible that God's character is most clearly portrayed.

Inspiration is also instrumental in revealing the presence and character of God's Son throughout the OT. This is especially seen in the way NT writers, through inspiration, bring out an abundance of new insights about Christ in the OT prophecies.[57]

To perfect the character of God's people. Ellen White frequently refers to the role of inspired Scripture in the development of a perfect character. She states that "'Given by inspiration of God,' able to make us 'wise unto salvation,' rendering the man of God 'perfect, thoroughly furnished unto all good works' (2 Tim 3:15-17), the Bible has the highest claim to our reverent attention."[58]

Commenting on 2 Timothy 3:16, 17, "All Scripture is given by inspiration of God, and is profitable for doctrine, for reproof, for correction, for instruction in righteousness: that the man of God may be perfect, thoroughly furnished unto all good works," she says: "In the Word of God is contained everything essential to the perfecting of the man of God. It is like a treasure-house, full of valuable and precious stores; but we do not appreciate its riches, nor realize the necessity of equipping ourselves with the treasures of truth."[59] "Its teaching will perfect in each individual a character that God can approve."[60] "Those who are defective in character, in conduct, in habits and practices, are to take heed to counsel and reproof."[61]

---

56   *Patriarchs and Prophets,* 596.
57   *Desire of Ages,* 413.
58   *Counsels to Parents, Teachers, and Students,* 139; *Messages to Young People,* 284.
59   "Benefits of Bible Study," *Bible Echo,* October 1, 1892, 290.
60   *Kress Collection,* 98.
61   "Words to the Young," *Youth's Instructor,* August 31, 1893, 276.

To make the Bible profitable. As the whole Bible is given by inspiration of God, every part of it is profitable. This implies that "the Old Testament no less than the New should receive attention. As we study the Old Testament we shall find living springs bubbling up where the careless reader discerns only a desert."[62]

How profitable are the accounts of Noah, Lot, Moses, Abraham, David, Solomon, Elijah, Jonah, Peter, Paul, Barnabas and others when all their faults and follies are recorded by "the pen of Inspiration"? The faithful portrayal of their failures and victories is given for our encouragement. Their experiences are intended as "a lesson to all the generations following them." Without this record of their weaknesses these heroes of faith "would have been more than human, and our sinful natures would despair of ever reaching such a point of excellence. But seeing where they struggled and fell, where they took heart again and conquered through the grace of God, we are encouraged, and led to press over the obstacles that degenerate nature places in our way."[63]

So profitable and far-reaching does she see the Bible's inspired teachings that, "practically carried out," they "will fit men for any position of duty."[64] She encourages believers in the daily study of the Scriptures, like the Bereans, to develop competence in using the words of inspiration, so that in confronting opposition we "like Christ," can meet "scripture with scripture."[65]

To provide the foundation for Christian education. Ellen White's interest in Christian education led her to emphasize the role of the inspired Word of God in schools. In commenting on the usefulness of inspired writings versus secular text books, she says, "To discard many of the worldly text-books will not lower the standard of education, but will raise it to a higher plane." Commenting on 2 Timothy 3:16, 17 she remarks, "If this is the breadth and depth of the Scriptures, shall we not lift the standard by making the word of God the

---

62 *Education,* 191.
63 *Testimonies,* 4:12. See also "Bible Bible Biographies," *Review and Herald,* January 22, 1880, 49.
64 *Testimonies,* 4:441.
65 *Gospel Workers,* 92, 124.

foundation of our system of education?"[66] She deplored at one time the lack of prominence the Bible received in the church's schools: "The Lord has been greatly dishonored in our institutions of learning when His Word has been made only a book among books. The very Book that contains infallible wisdom has scarcely been opened as a study book..."[67]

Evidences of Divine Inspiration

What is the evidence for the inspiration of the Scriptures? The evidences are seen in the biblical records themselves. Diligent study of the Bible results in the clearest conviction of its inspiration. Ellen White's major references to proofs of inspiration pertain to the mysteries and difficulties of the Bible, the magnificence of its themes, its prophecies and the unity of the Old and New Testaments.

"Divine inspiration" Ellen White writes, "asks many questions which the most profound scholar cannot answer. These questions were not asked that we might answer them, but to call our attention to the deep mysteries of God and to teach us that our wisdom is limited; that in the surroundings of our daily life there are many things beyond the comprehension of finite beings."[68]

Skeptics in their arguments against the inspiration of the Bible frequently point to the difficulties in the Bible. In response Ellen White observes that "the mysteries of the Bible, so far from being an argument against it, are among the strongest evidences of its divine inspiration." She adds that "if it contained no account of God but that which we could comprehend; if His greatness and majesty could be

---

66 "Instruction Regarding the School Work," *The General Conference Bulletin*, April 24, 1901, 452, 453.

67 Manuscript Releases, 11:171. She says, "The word of God is the most perfect educational book in our world. Yet in our colleges and schools, books produced by human intellect have been presented for the study of our students, and the Book of books, which God has given to men to be an infallible guide, has been made a secondary matter. Human productions have been used as most essential and the word of God has been studied simply to give flavor to other studies." *Fundamentals of Christian Education*, 394, 395.

68 *Ministry of Healing*, 431.

grasped by finite minds, then the Bible would not, as now, bear the unmistakable evidences of divinity."[69]

She refers to Peter's statement that there are in Scripture "things hard to be understood, which they that are unlearned and unstable wrest... unto their own destruction." These difficulties, she says, "constitute a strong evidence of its divine inspiration."[70] Thus instead of weakening our faith "the greatness of its themes should inspire faith in it as the word of God."[71]

The fulfillment of prophecy she presents as another evidence of the Bible's divine inspiration. Reports of the exact, historical fulfillment of prophecies have been instrumental in convincing skeptics and rationalists of the inspiration of the Bible.[72]

A careful study of the link between the Old and New Testaments gives additional proof of inspiration. "The more we study the Old and New Testaments," she states, "the more we shall have impressed on our mind the fact that each sustains a very close relation to the other, and the more evidence we shall receive of their divine inspiration. We shall see clearly that they have but one Author."[73]

Doubting the Inspiration of Scripture

The evidences of divine inspiration are abundant. Yet despite this many have difficulties in accepting the Bible as the true Word of God. Their minds are filled with questions and doubts. Why is there such a lack of conviction about the inspiration of the Bible? What are the deeper reasons for doubting inspiration? What are its results?

Causes for Doubting

Before dealing with the precise reasons for doubting the inspiration of the Bible we should recall that God, in His great love for

---

69 *Education*, 170.
70 *Testimonies*, 5:700; *Steps to Christ*, 107.
71 *Education*, 170.
72 *Great Controversy*, 364. Here she refers to Gaussen's experience with reading the fulfillment of Daniel 2 in Rollin's Ancient History.
73 *Selected Messages*, 3:359.

humans, has given them the freedom of choice. This is a fundamental principle of the Christian faith. Ellen White states clearly the choice that God gives: "Those who think it a virtue to quibble can have plenty of room to disbelieve the inspiration and truths of God's word. God does not compel any to believe. They can choose to rely upon the evidences He has been pleased to give, or doubt, and cavil, and perish."[74]

What are the reasons for doubt? Primarily, she says, they are related to people's relationship with God in terms of their attitudes and lifestyle. The difficulties about inspiration are not so much with by the Bible "as with their own hearts." The problem, she says, is that "the requirements of God's word are too close for their unsanctified natures. 'The carnal mind is enmity against God: for it is not subject to the law of God, neither indeed can be' [Rom 8:7]." When the natural heart is not subjected to "the sanctifying influence of the grace of God received through the channel of faith, the thoughts of the heart are not pure and holy."[75]

Foremost responsible for doubt, therefore, is the cherishing of sin in the life. She observes that "those who love sin will turn away from the Bible, will love to doubt, and will become reckless in principle. They will receive and advocate false theories."[76] "Those who have an evil heart of unbelief, will doubt, and will think it noble and a virtue to doubt the word of God."[77]

The underlying cause that fuels doubt is an unchristian lifestyle. "In almost every case, where persons become unsettled in regard to the inspiration of the word of God, it is on account of their unsanctified lives, which that word condemns. They will not receive its reproofs and threatenings because these reflect upon their wrong course of action."[78]

---

74   *Spiritual Gifts*, 4b:123; *Testimonies*, 1:377.
75   *Testimonies*, 1:440.
76   Ibid., 1:441.
77   *Spiritual Gifts*, 4b:123; *Testimonies*, 1:377.
78   *Testimonies*, 1:440. She adds: "Difficulties and doubts which perplex the vicious heart will be cleared away before the one practicing the pure principles of truth."

Finally she points to the absence of Christian virtues among believers as a cause for doubt. The lack of the grace of God, forbearance, patience, spirit of consecration and sacrifice, devotion, personal piety and holiness is frequently "the only reason why some are doubting the evidences of God's word."[79]

Results of Doubting. Ellen White vividly portrays the baneful consequence of the course of doubt. Doubt results in "lessening faith in the inspiration of the Bible."[80] It has a devastating influence on the mind and brings the doubter into the presence of evil angels.[81] She warns against expressing even a single word of doubt for it will do its damage. Satan will use it to "encourage skepticism" and turn believers "from the narrow path that leads to heaven." Suggestions of doubt, therefore, "weaken faith" and "confuse the perception of truth."[82]

Having started on the path of doubt, skeptics substitute the plain authoritative "Thus says the Lord" for "some winding sophistry of error." Instead of "the call of the Good Shepherd" they "follow the voice of strangers." Thus "infidelity has increased in proportion as men have questioned the word and requirements of their Maker."[83]

Doubters of inspiration are not satisfied to keep their thoughts to themselves. They are caught in an evangelistic zeal to spread their doubts and their questionings that will diminish faith in inspiration and make "shipwreck of the happiness of their fellow-men." Their zeal is in proportion to the amount of error they have imbibed: "The more they drifted into error, the greater grew their desire to draw other souls into the same channel of darkness."[84]

Protection against Doubts. As in nearly every case an "unsanctified" lifestyle causes people to doubt inspiration, it follows that practicing the biblical lifestyle is the antidote to doubt. Ellen White wri-

79　*Testimonies,* 1:383-384.
80　"The Faith that Will Stand the Test," *Review and Herald,* January 10, 1888, 18.
81　*Testimonies,* 1:427-428.
82　"The Faith that Will Stand the Test," *Review and Herald,* January 10, 1888, 18.
83　Ibid.
84　Ibid.

tes, "Difficulties and doubts which perplex the vicious heart will be cleared away before the one practicing the pure principles of truth."[85]

Purity of lifestyle Ellen White sees as the best way to protect believers against doubting inspiration: "Purity of life imparts refinement, which will lead those possessing it to shrink more and more from coarseness and indulgence in sin. Such will not be led away from the truth or be given up to doubt the inspiration of the word of God." But protection is not the only benefit. As a result of a pure lifestyle, they become a witness to the positive influence of inspiration: "They will engage in the daily study of the sacred word with ever-increasing interest, and the evidences of Christianity and inspiration will stamp their impress on the mind and life."[86]

In demonstrating what the study of the Bible can do to one's views of inspiration, Ellen White refers to William Miller. Here was a deist with no faith in the Scriptures, who, after a thorough study became fully convinced they were divinely inspired. This discovery had such an impact that it influenced the rest of his life, and he became God's special instrument in drawing the attention of the world to Christ's soon return.[87]

As a further protection against views that undermine confidence in inspiration, Ellen White calls for the establishment of denominational schools. "If we do not have schools for our youth," she says, "they will attend other seminaries and colleges, and will be exposed to infidel sentiments, to cavilings and questionings concerning the inspiration of the Bible."[88][88] This implies a grave responsibility to guard the Adventist educational system from unbiblical sentiments about inspiration. If this fails, church-related schools will be a danger instead of a blessing.

Finally, she warns against ministers who express doubts about the inspiration of the Bible. "I saw that however strongly men may have advocated the truth, however pious they may appear to be, when they begin to talk unbelief in regard to some scriptures, claiming that they

---

85   *Testimonies*, 1:440.
86   Ibid., 1:441.
87   *Spirit of Prophecy*, 4:205.
88   *Special Testimonies on Education*, (1897), 200-201.

cause them to doubt the inspiration of the Bible, we should be afraid of them, for God is at a great distance from them."[89]

Erroneous Views on Inspiration

There exist several views of inspiration. Each view, however, has a significant influence on the lifestyle of believers. What kinds of erroneous views and practices regarding inspiration does Ellen White especially warn against? What are the causes for these views? What are their results, and what impact do they have on Scripture?

A mix of inspired and uninspired writings. In 1884 a series of article in the Review and Herald advocated the idea that some things in the Scriptures are inspired and some not.[90] This view was endorsed and promoted by both the Battle Creek church and the college which was responsible for the training of church workers.

Ellen White strongly opposed this new view. Instead of providing new insights on inspiration, it did not have God's approval, because it criticized the Word of God. She explained: "God sets no man to pronounce judgment on His Word, selecting some things as inspired and discrediting others as uninspired."[91] Supporters of this view were walking on holy ground and "had better fear and tremble and hide their wisdom as foolishness."[92] Instead of being guided by Jesus, she said, "they have stepped before Jesus to show Him a better way than He has led us."[93]

Some found evidence for a partial inspiration of the Bible in the text by the translation rendered "All scripture given by inspiration of God" (2 Tim 3:16). This did not mean, she explained, that there is some Scripture that is not inspired. The text refers to the whole Bible. "The apostle means simply `I present to you the Living Oracles, the Scriptures, all given by inspiration of God,...'"[94]

---

89   *Testimonies,* 1:383-384.
90   G. I. B.,"Inspiration: Its Nature and Manner of Communication," Nos 1–10 in *Review and Herald,* January 8–June 3, 1884.
91   *Selected Messages,* 1:23. She adds that "the testimonies have been treated in the same way; but God is not in this."
92   Ibid., 1:23.
93   Ibid., 1:17.
94   "The Bible God's Inspired Word," *Bible Echo and Signs of the Times,* August. 26, 1895,

In her defense of the Bible Ellen White places the Word of God above criticism. "In giving the word," she writes, "'holy men of God spake as they were moved by the Holy Ghost.' The word was not given at the option of men, and the use to be made of it is not left to their option. Men may not dissect or pronounce upon, wrest or misinterpret, take from or cast aside, any portion of that word according to their own judgment." Calling attention to its divine origin and thought,she says, "Although its compilation, preservation, and transmission have been committed to men, it is wholly divine in its origin and in the thoughts expressed. It may not be demerited and pronounced upon by finite minds, because of its transmission through human agents."[95]

Sources influence the quality of inspiration

Some entertain the idea that a non-inspired source of information from which the inspired writer may derive some information affects the quality of inspiration. This view Ellen White also rejects. The Bible writings are fully inspired no matter from what sources the writers may obtain some of their materials. Referring to Paul's admonitions based on reports from the family of Chloe, she asks, whether Paul who "was to watch for souls as one that must render account to God," should "not take notice of the reports concerning their state of anarchy and division?" She answers "Most assuredly; and the reproof he sent them was written just as much under the inspiration of the Spirit of God as were any of his epistles." Those who refused his testimony "took the position that God had not spoken to them through Paul, that he had merely given them his opinion as a man, and they regarded their own judgment as good as that of Paul."[96] Thus God's inspired message was made of none effect.

Causes of the erroneous views and attitudes

The problem with those who designate some sections of the Bible as divine and others as human is that they fail to understand its divine nature. Ellen White observes that they neglect to see that "Christ, the divine, partook of our human nature, that He might reach humanity.

---

268. Emphasis hers.
95   *Bible Echo and Signs of the Times* August 26, 1995/01
96   *Testimonies,* 5:684.

In the work of God for man's redemption, divinity and humanity are combined."[97] As it is not possible and profitable to unravel the mystery of the divine-human nature of Christ, so humans should avoid attempting to distinguish between divine and human aspects in Scripture.

Low views of inspiration are also caused by exalting human ideas and talents above divine wisdom and "forms and science, so- called, above the power of vital godliness."[98]

The results of the erroneous views

The heretical views on inspiration that were introduced in the Adventist church in the 1880's had a subtle and far reaching, destructive influence. It impacted the 1886 General Conference in Oakland, Ellen White recounts, and "since then has been at work like leaven, and the very same prejudice and irritation of spirit that was upon the Pacific Coast in a degree we find this side of the Rocky Mountains," influencing the 1888 Minneapolis General Conference.[99] She portrayed the effect as "disastrous, both upon the one engaged in it and upon those who accept it as a work from God" and "skepticism has been aroused in many minds" as to the nature of inspiration. Advocates of these new theories she characterizes as "finite beings, with their narrow, short-sighted views." They are biased because they are "affected in a greater or less degree by surrounding influences, and having hereditary and cultivated tendencies which are far from making them wise or heavenly-minded." The detrimental results of their practice of judging the Scripture on "what is divine and what is human" is seen in a selective use of Scripture which views certain passages as important because they are inspired, while other texts are not so important because they are not inspired.[100]

Ellen White very much deplored the publication of these ideas. "These sentiments should never have seen the light of day," she said

---

97   Ibid., 5:747.
98   *Manuscript Releases*, 2:104.
99   *1988 Materials*, 187-188.
100 *Testimonies*, 5:709.

because they "undermine all inspiration." She is even more distressed about the lack of spiritual discernment among the believers. "Have God's people put out their eyes," she asked, "that they cannot distinguish between truth and error, the sacred and the profane?"[101] She foresaw a fearful harvest. Instead of being new light "it will lead many souls astray, and will be a savor of death to some."[102]

Counsels on the Study of Inspiration

What recommendations does Ellen White have on the proper way to approach the subject of inspiration? What are the do's and don'ts? What are the proper methods and sources?

The Don'ts in the Study of Inspiration

A major warning is that humans are not authorized to analyze the Bible to determine what is inspired and what is not. Addressing the Adventist ministry she warns, "My brethren in the ministry. 'Put off thy shoes from off thy feet, for the place whereon thou standest is holy ground.' [Exodus 3:5] There is no finite man that lives, I care not who he is or whatever is his position, that God has authorized to pick and choose in His Word."[103]

In addition she warns not to make a distinction in Scripture between revelation and inspiration: "Do not let any living man come to you and begin to dissect God's Word, telling what is revelation, what is inspiration and what is not, without a rebuke. Tell all such they simply do not know."[104] The reason she gives is that humans "simply are not able to comprehend the things of the mystery of God."[105] Her strong objections are connected to the practical consequences of making such a distinction. It will tend to undermine people's faith in the entire Bible as it reads. She says, "What we want is to inspire faith.

---

101 *1888 Materials*, 258.
102 *Manuscript Releases*, 7:382; *Manuscript Releases*, 12:367.
103 *Bible Commentary*, 7:919.
104 Ibid.
105 Ibid.

We want no one to say, 'This I will reject, and this will I receive,' but we want to have implicit faith in the Bible as a whole and as it is."[106]

Finally she cautions against associating with ministers, no matter how godly they seem, who display doubt on the inspiration of Scripture.[107]

The Do's in the Study of Inspiration

Christ's followers should approach the study of inspiration with a positive witness. In contrast to the views of low inspiration that exalt human ideas and talents, believers should affirm the divine inspiration of Scripture. "Let every one who believes in Jesus Christ," Ellen White says, "use his talent of voice in exalting Jesus and presenting testimonies that will magnify, honor, and adore the Word of God." The results of such a witness will be clearly visible for "the gospel makes itself known in its power in the consistent, holy, pure lives of those who are believers, hearers, and doers of the Word.[108]

To better understand the words of inspiration Ellen White recommends the study of her writings to the church. Addressing believers, she says "you are not familiar with the Scriptures" and "have neglected to acquaint yourselves with God's inspired Book." He "has sought to reach you by simple, direct testimonies, calling your attention to the words of inspiration which you had neglected to obey, and urging you to fashion your lives in accordance with its pure and elevated teachings."[109]

As to the role of these testimonies, she states, that they are not intended "to give new light, but to impress vividly upon the heart the truths of inspiration already revealed." She adds, "Additional truth is not brought out; but God has through the Testimonies simplified the great truths already given and in His own chosen way brought them before the people to awaken and impress the mind with them, that all may be left without excuse."[110]

---

106 Ibid.
107 *Testimonies*, 1:383-384.
108 *That I May Know Him*, 345.
109 *Testimonies*, 2:605; Ibid., 5:665.
110 Ibid., 2:695; Ibid., 5:665.

Conclusion

Ellen White's view of inspiration is in harmony with the high view of inspiration held by the Protestant Reformers who taught that the Bible, as the inspired Word of God, was the only infallible authority for faith and practice.

She saw inspiration as a process in which divine light was communicated to the human recipient and imparted to the people in a trustworthy manner. This process was a dynamic divine- human interaction in which the Holy Spirit moved upon the Bible writers. The style of the various Bible books reflects the individual writers who expressed the divine communications given by thoughts, dictations, visions, or dreams into human language. As weak and imperfect as these human beings and human language were, inspiration in the fullest sense of the word lifted these persons above their frailties so their human utterances became the infallible Word of God.

Biblical inspiration, therefore, makes the Bible God's special instrument for the salvation of humanity. It is His voice speaking to the soul, accurate and fully trustworthy; the infallible, unerring guide and rule for believers to lead them into a saving union with Christ and to assist them in a victorious lifestyle to prepare them to meet the Lord at His return.

It is not surprising that Satan's major target in the last days is the Scriptures. "Satan," she says, "is moving with his power from beneath to inspire men to form alliances and confederacies of evil against light and against the Word of God." One of the signs of the last days is the low views of inspiration and the exaltation of human ideas.[111]

Stressing the seriousness of the situation for Seventh-day Adventists, Ellen White notes that it affects the very foundation of the Bible. She says: "Never was there a stronger combination formed to neutralize the lesson and teachings of Christ, and to sow the seeds of infidelity in regard to the inspiration of the Scriptures and sap its very foundation."[112]

---

111 *That I May Know Him*, 345.
112 *Manuscript Releases*, 2:163.

She challenges apathetic believers by saying, "It is time we were endowed with power from on high." Fearing for the ability of believers to resist the darkness that is coming upon the earth, she confronts them with the searching question; "Where is the light and the power which shall withstand this terrible incoming darkness which is covering the world like a funeral pall?"[113]

"One of the marked signs of the last days," she asserts, is that "human reasoning and the imaginings of the human heart" are "undermining the inspiration of the Word of God." "There are in many churches skepticism and infidelity in the interpretation of the Scriptures. Many, very many, are questioning the verity and truth of the Scriptures." As a result "that which should be received as granted, is surrounded with a cloud of mysticism. Nothing stands out in clear and distinct lines, upon rock bottom."[114]

Attempts to unsettle minds regarding the correct view of inspiration will spread, she says, "until we may see the full meaning of the words of Christ, 'When the Son of man cometh, shall he find faith on the earth?' (Luke 18:8)."[115]

Recent church publications reveal a trend to introduce new approaches to the topic of inspiration. Although written with a noble purpose of assisting perplexed believers and affirming the inspiration of the Scriptures, they seem to add to the confusion. These approaches present concepts or definitions of inspiration and revelation that are not supported by Ellen White. They are simply modifications of the attempts made during the 1880's to distinguish between the divine and human nature of the Bible—an approach she strongly opposed. As long as her views on this subject are not taken seriously, the disunity among believers will continue to grow with all its negative consequences.

An unfortunate by-product of the current confusion is its inevitable negative impact on the believers' confidence in the infallibility of the Bible, which in turn, weakens faith in its doctrines, including that of the assurance of salvation. Ellen White sees an intimate connection

---

113 Ibid.
114 *Selected Messages*, 1:15. See also *The Faith I Live By*, 13. 115 *Selected Messages*, 1:17.
115 *Selected Messages*, 1:17.

between the true view of inspiration, the infallibility of the Scriptures and the absolute confidence in the trustworthiness of its teachings. This, therefore, makes it of paramount importance for church leaders to strive to uphold the true Biblical teaching of inspiration. It is vital to the believers' possession of the assurance of salvation and the effectiveness of their mission.

2

Ellen White on Theology: Its Methods, and the Use of Scripture

Seventh-day Adventists consider Ellen White (1827-1915) one of the founders of the Seventh-day Adventist Church and its most influential writer. The following discussion focuses on how she views theology, theological method, and its use in advancing divine truth. First we will look at her attitude toward theology. Then we will investigate what she has to say about theological methods.

Ellen White distinguishes two types of theology. The theology she approves of she calls "true" or "sound" theology. Theology she warns against is popular or objectionable theology.

Ellen White's Attitude Toward Theology

Characteristics of True Theology

Ellen White would like to see "in every school" a theology characterized by "the most simple theory."[1] The Bible contains a "system of theology and philosophy" that is both "simple and complete,"[2] yet "sublime."[3] It is so profoundly simple that even a child can understand it. Yet at the same time, so profoundly sublime that it baffles the intellectual giant.[4]

Originally published in the Journal of the Adventist Theological Society, 4/2 (1993): 115-136. Used with permission.

1   MS 156, 1898 (*Evangelism*, 223).
2   *Special Testimonies on Education*, 53
3   *That I May Know Him*, 8; see "The Bible a Means of Both Mental and Moral Culture," *Review and Herald*, Se 25, 1883.
4   Ibid.

Scripture's "grand central theme" consists of "God's original purpose for the world, of the rise of the great controversy, and of the work of redemption."[5] The "central truth" of a vital theology is the "atonement of Christ;" thus, students will be exposed to "the wonderful theme of redemption."[6] Its purpose is to make "us wise unto salvation." It reveals "the love of God as shown in the plan of redemption" and provides the essential knowledge of Christ as our Savior.[7]

A vital theology is to be "saturated with the love of Christ." Its effect produces in believers a practical wholistic lifestyle: The diffusion of this love throughout the body "touches every vital part,—the brain, the heart, the helping hands, the feet," enabling people to stand firmly for God.[8] It brings true vitality to the church and leads "to the doing of works that will bear fruit after the similitude of the character of God."[9]

True theology, as stated by Wycliffe, centers around the "distinctive doctrines of Protestantism—salvation through faith in Christ, and the sole infallibility of the Scripture."[10] It continues the process of reform that began with the Protestant Reformation to lead people away from a dependence on human and ecclesiastical traditions. Among proponents who gave leadership to a vital theology she lists individuals in the Reformation heritage such as Wycliffe,[11] Luther,[12] Zwingli[13] and Wesley.[14] This she places in sharp contrast to Satan's strategy in directing people's attention to the "opinions of learned men, the deductions of science, the creeds or decisions of ecclesiastical councils,... the voice of the majority" for deciding what is truth for faith.[15]

---

5   *Education,* 190.
6   MS 156, 1898 (*Evangelism,* 223).
7   *Special Testimonies on Education,* 53. See also, *Counsels to Parents, Students and Teachers,* 422; *Fundamentals of Christian Education,* 129.
8   "Principles of Service," *Signs of the Times,* May 10, 1910.
9   "What God Is," *Southern Review,* January 1, 1901.
10 *Great Controversy,* 89; cf. Ibid., 102.
11 Ibid., 79-96.
12 Ibid., 120-170. Luther's hope for the success of true theology was the younger, not the older generation for they had not yet been educated in error (Ellen G. White, "Summoned to Augsburg," *Signs of the Times,* June 28, 1983).
13 *Great Controversy,* 171-184.
14 Ibid., 253-264.
15 Ibid., 595.

Characteristics of Popular Theology

Popular theology is characterized by false interpretations of Scripture. The origin of many of these errors may be traced to the ages of papal darkness, that is the Dark Ages.[16]

The nature of this theology is speculative. It exalts human theories based on philosophy and theology above the Word of God and stands in sharp contrast to the eternal truths taught by the Bible writers.[17] Its presence is widespread. To a large degree, Ellen White writes, theology, as studied and taught, is but a record of human speculation.[18]

Objectionable theology mixes religion with harmful amusements. She specifically rejects a theology which advocates that it is necessary for the health of patients to play cards and dance as a "pleasurable excitement to keep their spirits u"[19]

Major errors. Throughout her writings she comments on many errors in popular theology. Among the most prominent are the doctrine of natural immortality,[20] the ministering spirits of the dead,[21] the everlasting punishing in hell,[22] the consciousness of the dead,[23] the transference of the biblical day of worship from Sabbath to Sunday,[24] and the abolition of God's moral law, the Decalogue.[25]

Results of erroneous theology. The problem with erroneous theology is its detrimental effects on mind and judgment which exposes believers to temptations. The study of these speculations confuses the mind.[26] Says Ellen White, it perverts the judgment and opens the door to temptation, and through its influence Satan seeks to turn hearts from the truth." For a defense she recommends "an intelligent love

---

16 *Testimonies,* 5:710,711.

17 Great Controversy, 126. See also Ellen G. White, "Luther at Wittenberg," Signs of the Times, June 7, 1883.

18 *Counsels to Teachers,* 380.

19 *Manuscript Releases,* 5:380. This view was the result of the theology of Dr. Jackson.

20 *Great Controversy,* 551.

21 Ibid.

22 *Spirit of Prophecy,* 4:356.

23 *The Faith I Live By,* 174 ; White, Great Controversy, 546.

24 *1888 Materials,* 780.

25 *Great Controversy,* 260-264 .

26 *Counsels to Teachers,* 380.

for the truth" which "sanctifies the receiver, and keeps him from the enemy's deceptive snares."[27]

The theological errors which were introduced into the church during the ages of papal supremacy had a devastating effect. They created "an erroneous conception of God"[28] which led many to doubt and skepticism about the Bible as the Word of God.[29] "Thousands upon thousands" have become skeptics and unbelievers.[30]

Unsound theology confuses the intellect and disqualifies a person for teaching. Speaking of Dr. Kellogg, she says, his "theology is not sound; his mind is confused, and unless he sees his danger, his foundation will be swept away when the test comes. Unless he sees his danger and makes a decided change, he can not be endorsed as a safe, all-round teacher."[31]

Incorrect approaches. There are two dangers against which Ellen White especially warns. One is a "scientific theology" which had come into the Battle Creek church in 1906. Its impact led people away from a true faith in God and raised questions about her writings.[32]

The second danger is the work of higher criticism, also called historical criticism. It is the use of the historical-critical method for the study of the Bible. This approach she characterizes as "dissecting, conjecturing, reconstructing" the Scriptures. The result is the destruction of faith in Scripture as the Word of God.[33] She considered it to be one of Satan's tools of deception. Through its "pleasing sentiments," she says, "the enemy of righteousness is seeking to lead souls into forbidden paths."[34]

---

27   "The Christian Pathway," *Signs of the Times,* March 6, 1884.
28   *Testimonies,* 5:710,711.
29   *Great Controversy,* 525.
30   *Testimonies,* 5:710,711.
31   *Battle Creek Letters,* 87.
32   "Hold Fast the Beginning of Your Confidence," *Review and Herald,* August 9, 1906. See *The Paulson Collection of Ellen G. White Letters,* 66; White, MS 61, June 3, 1906.
33   *Education,* 227.
34   *Acts of the Apostles,* 474. His other tools are "evolution, spiritualism, theosophy, and pantheism (Ibid.).

The reason for her strong opposition to higher criticism is that it "is destroying faith in the Bible as a divine revelation; it is robbing God's word of power to control, uplift, and inspire human lives."[35] She compares its influence to the destructive effect of tradition and rabbinical teaching in Christ's days.[36]

In a sermon she ironically contrasts the higher critics, whom she identifies as "poor, finite man on probation," with the true Higher Critic, "the Lord God of the universe who has spread the canopy of the heavens above us, and has made the stars and called them forth in their order."[37]

Motives for Studying Theology

Too often the study of theology is pursued with an incorrect motive: "An ambition to become acquainted with philosophers and theologians, a desire to present Christianity to the people in learned terms and propositions."[38] This is contrary to the true theology of Scripture with its emphasis on clarity and plainness.

Correct motives are directed by a desire to nourish food for both mind and soul.[39] When it comes to motives for studying theology in non-SDA institutions Ellen White calls attention to the motives of the Waldenses studying in Roman Catholic institutions. The purpose of their study was evangelistic: sowing "the seeds of truth in other minds" while getting an education. However, this mission was not for all young people and leadership is to hand pick those qualified. It was only for those who possessed the special spiritual qualifications: "Strong young men, rooted and grounded in the faith" with "a living connection with God."[40]

Today's objectives for such a study would be similar: Students "would have a wider field for study and observation," be associa-

35 Education, 227.
36 Ministry of Healing, 142.
37 MS 43a, 1894.
38 Ministry of Healing, 442.
39 Ibid.
40 Testimonies, 5:583, 584; Ellen G. White, Mind, Character, and Personality, 1:354.

ted "with different classes of minds," and obtain "an acquaintance with the workings and results of popular methods of education, and a knowledge of theology as taught in the leading institutions of learning." This education will prepare students for the specific mission of laboring for "the educated classes" as well as combating "the prevailing errors of our time."[41]

The Objectives of Theology

Researching and interpreting the Bible is a delicate occupation. Ellen White points out that "all who handle the word of God are engaged in a most solemn and sacred work."[42] The objectives of this important work that Ellen White sees follow.

Use Correct Principles of Interpretation

One of the foremost objectives for those engaged in theology is finding the correct principles to interpret the Bible. These principles are found in "the Bible and the Bible only." There students will discover the vital principle that "the Bible is its own interpreter."[43] This principle she fully endorses in her account of the conflict between the Protestant reformers and the papacy.[44] The principle of the Bible interpreting itself, one part of Scripture interprets another [45] within its own biblical context [46] is basic for all interpretation.

Acquire Sound Wisdom

A correct interpretation of Scripture requires the possession of sound wisdom. This wisdom comes only with much personal effort. "We cannot obtain wisdom without earnest attention and prayerful study."[47] The study of Scripture generates the quality of wisdom necessary for successful discovery of truth.

---

41   *Testimonies*, 5:584.
42   MS 4, 1896 in *Manuscript Releases*, 4:55.
43   See e.g., *Great Controversy*, 173. cf. *Testimonies to Ministers*, 106.
44   *Fundamentals of Education*, 187.
45   *Child Guidance*, 511.
46   See *Great Controversy*, 102, 126, 132, 173.
47   *Christian Education*, 58.

Search for Salvation

God desires that all should obtain salvation. This salvation "depends on a knowledge of the truth contained in the Scriptures." It is, therefore, obvious that one of the most important tasks of individuals engaged in theology is to "search the precious Bible with hungry hearts."[48]

The Bible, she remarks, "contains the science of all sciences, the science of salvation."[49] The quest for truth, therefore, should never sto "The more we study the Word with a simple, trustful heart, the more we understand the path we must travel in order to reach the Paradise of God."[50]

Study Qualifies for Soul-winning

Again and again we are impressed with Ellen White's stress on the practicality of Bible research. The gospel truths must be shared.[51] It is through digging "deep in the Scriptures of truth," with weeping, fasting and praying that a person becomes qualified "to go forth and watch for souls as they that must give an account."[52] Thus Bible study is crucial in the development of soul-winning strategies.

Concentrate on the Biblical Text

Another objective of theology is to understand the biblical text. Ellen White encourages a search to discover the meaning of difficult passages. Some Scriptural passages "are easily understood," but "the true meaning of other parts is not so readily discerned."[53] This underscores the need for serious Bible study so as to grasp the meaning of these difficult passages.

There is the need to discover the deeper meaning of Bible passages. In the words of Scripture there lies a significance that must be discovered, going beyond the surface. In reflecting on Christ as "the

---

48   *Christ's Object Lessons,* 111.
49   Ibid., 107.
50   *Upward Look,* 54.
51   See MS 4, 1896 in *Manuscript Releases,* 4:55, 56.
52   "My People Have Committed Two Evils," *Signs of the Times,* October 2, 1893.
53   *Testimonies to Ministers,* 108.

truth," she says, "His words are truth, and they have a deeper significance than appears on the surface."[54]

Ellen White warns against a shallow understanding of the truth.
"We must not be satisfied with superficial knowledge," but "seek to
learn the full meaning of the words of truth, and to drink deep of the
spirit of the holy oracles."[55] This enterprise, demands "careful thought
as to the meaning of the sacred text."[56] Much searching of the Bible,
therefore, is an indispensable requirement for its understanding.

Understand the Historical-Cultural Setting

A realistic picture of the historical, cultural context of biblical
episodes leads to an improved understanding of both the past and the
present. To achieve this Ellen White suggests going back in our minds
to the original scene. She illustrates this by an episode from the life of
Christ, inviting the readers to "enter into the thoughts and feelings" of
His disciples. "Understanding what the words of Jesus meant to those
who heard them we may discern in them a new vividness and beauty,
and may also gather for ourselves their deep lessons."[57] In doing so,
Ellen White does not endorse the view that the key to the knowledge
of the Bible is its socio-cultural context of the surrounding religious,
political, and social institutions. The proper and supreme context of
the Bible for understanding is the revelation of God embodied in the
Bible itself.

Separate Truth from Errors

Ellen White challenges the researcher to rescue God's truth from
the erroneous interpretations that have accumulated throughout the
centuries: "There is a great work to be done by the earnest Bible student; for gems of truth are to be gathered up, and separated from the
companionship of error."[58] Errors have crept into theology over many
centuries, but the Bible will be the guide to separate error from truth.
"There are errors and inconsistencies which many denounce as the

---

54   *Christ's Object Lessons,* 110. *See Christian Education,* 59; *Steps to Christ,* 90-91.
55   "Search the Scriptures," *Review and Herald,* October 9, 1883.
56   Ibid.
57   *Thoughts from the Mount of Blessing,* 1.
58   "The Bible Our Guide," *Bible Echo,* October 15, 1892.

teaching of the Bible that are really false interpretations of Scripture, adopted during the ages of papal darkness."[59] What looks like an inconsistency or error does not seem to be one in fact for those who "cling to the Bible as it reads, and stop... criticisms in regard to its validity."[60]

Bible Study: Medium of Communication

Ellen White says that "the Bible is the mine of the unsearchable riches of Christ."[61] She encourages digging deep into this most precious mine to gather its magnificent gems. "The study of the Scriptures is the means divinely ordained to bring men into closer connection with their Creator, and to give them a clearer knowledge of His will." Such study "is the medium of communication between God and man."[62]

Avoid Criticism: Affirm God's Character

In colorful terms she addresses those trying "to correct the errors of the Bible:" "In seeking to make plain or unravel mysteries hid for ages from mortal man, they are like a man floundering about in the mud, unable to extricate himself and yet telling others how to get out of the muddy sea they themselves are in."[63] Confidently she adds, "No man can improve the Bible by suggesting what the Lord meant to say or ought to have said."[64] Instead of criticizing the Bible we must reveal to the world God's true character.[65]

Recognize Unfolding Nature of Scripture

Bible truth is progressive. It "is an advancing truth."[66] It is true that "we have some understanding of the inspired books of the Old and New Testament," but "there is much that even in our day we do not

---

59   *Testimonies,* 5:710.
60   *Selected Messages,* 1:18.
61   *Christ's Object Lessons,* 107.
62   *Great Controversy,* 69.
63   *Selected Messages,* 1:16.
64   Ibid.
65   *Testimonies,* 5:710.
66   *Counsels to Writers and Editors,* 33.

see and comprehend."[67] There is "need of deep research"[68] to discover "new aspects of truth in both the Old and New Testament," and see "the exceeding breadth and compass of truths which we imagine we understand, but of which we have only a superficial knowledge."[69]

There is a "need for thorough and continuous searching of the Scriptures for greater light. We must watch with earnestness that we may discern any ray of light which God shall present to us."[70] "We are to catch the first gleamings of truth," she says, that "through prayerful study clearer light may be obtained, which can be brought before others."[71] It is God's will that His people "should be ever moving forward, to receive the increased and ever-increasing light which is shining for them."[72] "We must walk in the increasing light."[73] It is obvious that the new light and advanced truth brings new responsibilities that will profoundly effect the behavior and mission of the church.

Examine the Foundations of Our Faith

Ellen White indicates that the new light God has given to Seventh-day Adventists should "lead us to a diligent study of the Scriptures, and a most critical examination of the positions which we hold. God would have all the bearings and positions of truth thoroughly and perseveringly searched, with prayer and fasting." Its purpose being that the believers' faith should "be firmly founded upon the word of God so that when the testing time shall come and they are brought before councils to answer for their faith they may be able to give a reason for the hope that is in them, with meekness and fear."[74]

Ellen White encourages an open-minded attitude towards the traditional Seventh-day Adventist interpretations, saying that "there is no excuse for anyone in taking the position that there is no more truth

---

67   "Imperative Necessity of Searching for Truth," *Review and Herald,* Nov. 15, 1892.
68   Ibid.
69   "Bible Our Guide."
70   *Testimonies,* 5:708.
71   Ibid.
72   Ibid., 708-709.
73   *Writers and Editors,* 33.
74   *Testimonies,* 5:708.

to be revealed, and that all our expositions of Scripture are without an error."[75]

She warns against the idea that all teachings of the church are infallible. The fact that certain doctrines have been held "as truth for many years by our people is not a proof that our ideas are infallible. Age will not make error into truth, and truth can afford to be fair. No true doctrine will lose anything by close investigation."[76] She says that "in closely investigating every jot and title which we think is established truth, in comparing scripture with scripture, we may discover errors in our interpretations of Scripture." She confidently promises that if such a "search is properly conducted, jewels of inestimable value will be found. The word of God is the mine of the unsearchable riches of Christ."[77]

"Truth is eternal," she says, "and conflict with error will only make manifest its strength... If the pillars of our faith will not stand the test of investigation, it is time that we knew it."[78] This "investigation," however, should follow the proper principles of interpretation.

Principles Underlying Methods of Theology

Ellen White bases the methods of theology on three characteristics of the Bible: uniqueness, authority and unity.

The Uniqueness of the Bible

Authorship. The Bible is different from all other books. Its uniqueness rests in its divine *authorship.* "The Bible," Ellen White says, "points to God as its author."[79] All its revealed truths are "given by inspiration of God" (2 Tim. 3:16). Yet this awareness does not come without thoughtful study. "The evidence of the truth of God's word is

---

75 "Christ Our Hope," *Review and Herald,* December 20, 1892; White, *Writers and Editors,* 35.

76 Ibid.

77 "Treasure Hidden," *Review and Herald,* July 12, 1898.

78 *Testimonies to Ministers,* 107.

79 *Great Controversy,* v.

in the word itself."[80] This means that one must become personally acquainted with the Bible. "A settled faith in the divinity of the Holy Scriptures," she writes, comes "through personal experience," in "a knowledge of God and His word."[81]

Infallibility and Trustworthiness. When theologians deal with the Bible they must have confidence in its accuracy and reliability. Assurance in its accuracy is associated with the understanding of inspiration. Ellen White views inspiration as a process. First, God qualifies persons to communicate His truth.[82] Then, He guides "the mind in the selection of what to speak and what to write."[83] She observes that the Bible has been written in human language and "everything that is human is imperfect."[84] But although God communicates His testimony "through the imperfect expression of human language, yet it is the testimony of God."[85] It is important not to forget the function of the Bible: It "was given for practical purposes."[86] Human language, therefore, imperfect though it may be, can still function as an accurate and trustworthy vehicle for communication of eternal truths.

The sacred text has been remarkably preserved by God throughout history in spite of the work of some copyists, who, influenced by tradition, when copies were few, have tried to improve the text "when in reality they were mystifying that which was plain."[87]

The Bible is "to be accepted as an authoritative, infallible revelation of His will."[88] "Man is fallible," she states, "but God's Word is infallible."[89] The Bible is "the unerring standard" by which all ideas must be tested.[90]

---

80   *Testimonies,* 8:157.
81   *Ministry of Healing,* 462.
82   *Selected Messages,* 1:26.
83   Ibid.
84   Ibid., 20.
85   Ibid., 26.
86   Ibid., 20.
87   *Early Writings,* 220-221.
88   *Great Controversy,* vii.
89   "A Missionary Appeal," *Review and Herald,* December 15, 1885.
90   *Ministry of Healing,* 462.

Ellen White rejects the claim that the Bible contains contradictions. Such a conclusion derives from a "superficial knowledge" of the Bible.[91] Rightly understood it reveals "perfect harmony."[92]

The Authority of the Bible

Source. Like its uniqueness, the authority of the Bible is rooted in God's authorship It is "God's voice speaking to us, just as surely as though we could hear it with our ears."[93] Consequently the Bible is the "only infallible authority in religion."[94] Humans are to receive it as the "supreme authority."[95]

Extent. Its authority extends over faith, doctrine, experience,[96] history,[97] science,[98] human wisdom,[99] and extra biblical revelation.[100] Ellen White always recognizes the Bible as the supreme norm by which everything, including her own works, ought to be tested.[101]

Although not in favor of creeds, she urges people to adopt a creed for their lives: "The Bible, and the Bible alone, is to be our creed."[102]

In speaking about the extent of its superiority, she states that "God's holy word needs not the torch light glimmer of earth to make its glories distinguishable," because "it is light in itself—the glory of God revealed, and beside it every other light is dim."[103] Therefore she warns: "Never let mortal man sit in judgment upon the Word of God."[104]

91 *Selected Messages,* 1:20.
92 *Christian Education,* 194.
93 *Testimonies,* 6:393.
94 See *Great Controversy,* 238. cf. Ibid. 177.
95 *Testimonies,* 6:402.
96 See *Great Controversy,* vii.
97 *Bible Echo,* August 1891; White, *Christian Education,* 65. Here she said that in the Bible only can we find "the history of our race unsullied by human prejudice or human pride."
98 *Fundamentals of Education ,* 181.
99 See *SDA Bible Commentary,* 6:1079.
100 *Selected Messages,* 2:85-100.
101 Ibid.
102 *Selected Messages,* 1:416.
103 *Christ's Object Lessons,* 111.
104 *SDA Bible Commentary,* 7:919.

This view has far reaching implications for the theological approach to Scripture. It means that a study of the Bible itself is far more valuable than the study of the great writers of theology.[105]

The Unity of the Bible

Fundamental to the unity of the Bible is its divine authorship[106] This view has profound implications on the nature and relationship of the books that make up the Scriptures.

Harmony of Scripture. A unique characteristic of the Bible is the harmony that exists between the books that compose it. Although written by various persons, each writer, "under the guidance of the Holy Spirit, presents what is most forcibly impressed upon his own mind—a different aspect of truth in each, but a perfect harmony through all."[107]

Many do not see this unity. First, it requires divine illumination. Ellen White points out that only "the illuminated soul sees a spiritual unity, one grand golden thread running through the whole but it requires patience, thought, and prayer to trace out the precious golden thread."[108] Second, biblical harmony is discovered through a thorough research of the Scripture. Said she, "He who earnestly searches the Scriptures will see that harmony exists between the various parts of the Bible; he will discover the bearing of one passage upon another, and the reward of his toil will be exceedingly precious."[109]

Progressive revelation. An understanding of the concept of progressive revelation as the unfolding of previous divine revelation is important in perceiving the unity of the Bible. This concept is a divine design that is carefully interwoven throughout the Scriptures. Ellen White writes that the Scriptures were given to men, not in a continuous chain of unbroken utterances, but piece by piece through successive generations, as God in His providence saw a fitting oppor-

---

105 "Bible Study," *Review and Herald,* January 11, 1881.
106 *Great Controversy,* v.
107 Ibid.
108 *Selected Messages,* 20.
109 "Bible Our Guide," cf. "Searching for Truth."

tunity to impress man at sundry times and divers places. Men wrote as they were moved upon by the Holy Ghost."[110]

Progressive revelation can be illustrated with the ancient prophets. They received special illumination from the Spirit, but they did not fully comprehend "the import of the revelations committed to them. The meaning was to be unfolded from age to age, as the people of God should need the instruction therein contained."[111] These new insights "unfolded from age to age" were always in full harmony with previous revelations.

Ellen White saw a striking example of progressive revelation in the relationship between the Old and New Testaments. She states: "The Old Testament is the gospel in figures and symbols. The New Testament is the substance. One is as essential as the other."[112] This intimate unity explains her statement that "the Savior is revealed in the Old Testament as clearly as in the New."[113] "The New Testament does not present a new religion; the Old Testament does not present a religion to be superseded by the New. The New Testament is only the advancement and unfolding of the Old."[114]

Divine revelation in the lives of the Bible writers brought about unique literary productions characterized by a harmonious unity in diversity, not uniformity. She wrote: "The Lord gave His word... through different writers, each having his own individuality. Each has an experience of his own, and this diversity broadens and deepens the knowledge that is brought out to meet the necessities of varied minds."[115] Consequently "the thoughts expressed have not a set uniformity, as if cast in an iron mold, making the very hearing monotonous. In such uniformity there would be a loss of grace and distinctive beauty."[116] The distinctiveness of the different Bible books are needed for the biblical message to penetrate human hearts.

---

110 *Selected Messages*, 1:19-20.
111 *Great Controversy*, 344.
112 *Selected Messages*, 2:104.
113 *Desire of Ages*, 799.
114 *Testimonies*, 6:392.
115 *Selected Messages*, 1:21-22.
116 Ibid., 22.

Limitations of Theology

Theology as practiced by human beings has serious limitations. "In the Word of God many queries are raised," Ellen White writes, "that the most profound scholars can never answer."[117] The reason for this is that the" word of God, like the character of its divine Author, presents mysteries that can never be fully comprehended by finite beings."[118] In the research of the Scriptures one may go as deep as possible, "and yet there is an infinity beyond."[119]

To keep human achievements in theology in their proper perspectives she brings out that it must "be emphasized, and often repeated, that the mysteries of the Bible are not because God has sought to conceal truth, but because our own weakness or ignorance makes us incapable of comprehending or appropriating truth. The limitation is not in His purpose but in our capacity."[120]

The differences between the finite creature and the infinite Creator should always be kept in mind by the researcher and interpreter. This difference, Ellen White says, makes it impossible "for created beings to attain to a full understanding of God and His works."[121] "The depth of human intellect may be measured; the works of human authors may be mastered; but the highest, deepest, broadest flight of the imagination cannot find out God. There is infinity beyond all that we can comprehend."[122]

Illustrating the magnitude and grandeur of the Word of God, she writes, "It is impossible for any human mind to exhaust even one truth or promise of the Bible. One catches the glory from one point of view, another from another point; yet we can discern only gleamings. The full radiance is beyond our vision. As we contemplate the great things of God's Word, we look into a fountain that broadens and deepens beneath our gaze. Its breadth and depth pass our knowledge.

---

117 Ibid., 3:310.
118 *Steps to Christ,* 106.
119 "Bible Study."
120 *Education,* 170.
121 "The Mysteries of the Bible a Proof of Its Inspiration," *Bible Echo,* July 15, 1889.
122 *Christ's Object Lessons,* 113.

As we gaze, the vision widens; stretched out before us we behold a boundless, shoreless sea."[123]

This view of human limitations should keep persons humble in their theological statements.

Proper Methods of Theology

Miller's Principles Endorsed

William Miller›s principles of interpretation, which underlie the foundations of SDA theology, Ellen White fully endorses. Said she: Those who are engaged in proclaiming the third angels message are searching the Scriptures upon the same plan that Father Miller adopted. His method consisted of simple but intelligent and important rules for Bible study and interpretation.[124]

The successful use of these methods is intimately connected with the exercise of genuine faith: "Nothing revealed in Scripture can or will be hid from those who ask in faith, not wavering."[125] Several of the following concepts can be found among Miller's principles.

Bible only

In light of the general departure from Bible truth Ellen White stresses the "need of a return to the great Protestant principle&emdash;the Bible, and the Bible only, as the rule of faith and duty."[126] She states that "searching the Scriptures alone will bring the knowledge of the true God and Jesus Christ whom He has sent."[127]

In the quest for an understanding of Bible truth it is not imperative to study extra-biblical sources while they may illuminate certain backgrounds, the divine revelation in the Scriptures is fully adequate. "All that man needs to know and can know of God," she says, "has

---

123 *Education*, 171.

124 "Notes of Travel," *Review and Herald*, Nov. 25, 1884.

125 Ibid.

126 *Great Controversy*, 204, 205.

127 *Fundamentals of Education*, 415.

been revealed in His Word and in the life of His Son, the great Teacher."[128]

The whole canon of the Scriptures should be the context in which the student operates. The student "should learn to view the Word as a whole, and to see the relation of its parts."[129] This view cautions against the practice of using a "canon within a canon" that draws conclusions from a constricted Bible in which a certain topic is elevated to function as most important theme at the expense of equally important other themes.

The Role of the Spirit of Prophecy

The relation between the Bible and the operation of the Spirit of Prophecy at the end of time (Rev 12:17; 19:10) is carefully defined. The Bible, Ellen White writes, assures true believers continual guidance by the Holy Spirit. God also has promised in the Bible to give "visions in the 'last days;' not for a new rule of faith, but for the comfort of His people, and to correct those who err from Bible truth."[130] The reason for this role of the Holy Spirit in the end-time is because "little heed is given to the Bible." Through the Spirit of Prophecy "the Lord has given a lesser light to lead men and women to the greater light."[131] Ellen White makes the following comparison: "In ancient times God spoke to men by the mouth of prophets and apostles. In these days He speaks to them by the testimonies of His Spirit."[132]

The Testimonies. What is the relation of Ellen White's messages or testimonies to the Bible? They are not an addition to the Bible, but an aid in its understanding. "God," she said, "has seen fit in this manner to bring the minds of His people to His word, to give them a clearer understanding of it."[133] They are not to give "new light" but "to impress vividly upon the heart the truths of inspiration already revealed." She emphasizes that "additional truth is not brought out; but God has through the Testimonies simplified the great truths already

---

128 MS 124, 1903 in *Bible Commentary,* 6:1079.
129 *Education,* 190.
130 *Early Writings,* 78.
131 "An Open Letter... ," *Review and Herald,* January 20, 1903.
132 *Testimonies,* 5:661.
133 Ibid., 663.

given and in His own chosen way brought them before the people to awaken and impress the mind with them, that all may be left without excuse."[134]

Although these testimonies are not new light, they contain light that corrects errors and defines truth: "The Lord has given me much light that I want the people to have for there is instruction that the Lord has given me for His people." She adds that "this is now to come before the people, because it has been given to correct specious errors and to specify what is truth."[135]

The establishment of the foundations of the Seventh-day Adventist Church shows the intimate relationship between the Bible and the Spirit of Prophecy. Often Ellen White's visions would confirm the results of the Bible studies of the Adventist Sabbathkeepers during the formative years. However, there were a few times when the Bible conferences were stalled and her visions broke the deadlock and guided the believers to the correct biblical solution. The truth—"especially concerning the ministration of Christ in the heavenly sanctuary, and the message of Heaven for these last days, as given by the angels of the fourteenth chapter of Revelation," she says, "has been sought out by prayerful study, and testified to by the miracle-working power of the Lord." It is God Himself, she declares, who "through His Word and the testimony of His Spirit" has revealed the permanence of these "fundamental principles that are based upon unquestionable authority."[136]

Definition of the "Bible only." An analysis of Ellen Whites use of the phrase «the Bible and the Bible only» reveals that she contrasts it with human views and ideas,[137] erroneous traditions on the Sabbath and the Law of God,[138] mistaken opinions of scholars, scientists,

---

134 Ibid., 665.
135 Letter 127, 1910 in *Selected Messages,* 3:32. The published source has a typographical error. It refers to Letter 117 instead of 127.
136 *Selected Messages,* 1:208.
137 "Missionary Appeal."
138 *Great Controversy,* 448.

theologians,[139] sayings and doings of men,[140] human wisdom,[141] false visions,[142] views of the churches steeped in popular theology from which the early Adventists separated themselves,[143] the religions of fable and tradition, imaginary religion, a religion of words and forms, and tradition and human theories and maxims.[144] These phrases show that she uses the «Bible only» to contrast biblical truth with the unbiblical positions of religious traditions, experience, ecclesiastical position and human reason.

The expression the "Bible only" was never contrasted with her own writings. In Ellen White's mind there was perfect harmony between the Bible and her writings because "the Holy Ghost is the author of the Scriptures and the author of the spirit of prophecy."[145] Therefore, "it is impossible that the teachings of the Spirit should ever be contrary to that of the word."[146]

This unique relationship between the Bible and the Spirit of Prophecy has given the latter a place above all extra-biblical sources. Consequently in the study of the Bible the writings of the Spirit of Prophecy (Ellen White) hold a superior position over other research tools. Ellen White maintains that her writings while in harmony with the Bible are not to be added to the Bible. As noted above she maintains that the Spirit of Prophecy writings are the "lesser light to lead men and women to the great light [the Bible]."

The Use of Non-Inspired Christian Writings

As to the religious value of non-inspired Christian sources, she says, "the opinions of learned men, the deductions of science, the creeds or decisions of ecclesiastical councils, as numerous and discordant as are the churches which they represent, the voice of the

---

139 Ibid, 595.
140 *Counsels on Sabbath Work*, 84.
141 *Fundamentals of Education*, 200.
142 *Selected Messages*, 2:85.
143 *Writers and Editors*, 145.
144 *Prophets and Kings*, 624-626.
145 Letter 92, 1900.
146 *Great Controversy*, vii.

majority,—not one nor all of these should be regarded as evidence for or against any point of religious faith."[147]

On the value of commentaries she remarks that "many think that they must consult commentaries on the Scriptures in order to understand the meaning of the word of God." She does not object to their use, stating, "We would not take the position that commentaries should not be studied," but cautions that "it will take much discernment to discover the truth of God under the mass of the words of men."[148] She says, "many think it essential to acquire an extensive knowledge of historical and theological writings" because "they suppose that this knowledge will be an aid to them in teaching the gospel" but "their laborious study of the opinions of men tends to the enfeebling of their ministry, rather than to its strengthening."[149]

Bible: Self-interpreting

Ellen White believes that Scripture is the key to understand Scripture and to unlock the treasure house of truth. She recommends Miller's rule: "Scripture must be its own expositor, since it is a rule of itself. If I depend on a teacher to expound it to me, and he should guess at its meaning, or desire to have it so on account of his sectarian creed, or to be thought wise, then his guessing, desire, creed, or wisdom, is my rule, not the Bible."[150]

In explaining her position she remarks, "we are not to accept the opinions of commentators as the voice of God" because "they were erring mortals like ourselves. God has given reasoning powers to us as well as to them. We should make the Bible its own expositor."[151] The operation of this method she places within the broad perspective of Christ's role within the great controversy between good and evil.[152]

Theological methods, therefore, must be derived from the Bible. The two following methods are the result of this rule.

---

147 See *Great Controversy*, 595.
148 *Fundamentals of Education*, 187-188.
149 *Ministry of Healing*, 441.
150 "Notes of Travel."
151 *Testimonies to Ministers*, 106.
152 See *Education*, 190.

The Analogy of Scripture

For the understanding and development of doctrine Ellen White endorses Millers method of the analogy of Scripture: «To understand doctrine, bring all the Scriptures together on the subject you wish to know, then let every word have its proper influence; and if you can form your theory without a contradiction, you cannot be in error."[153] This method teaches that to understand Bible doctrine correctly, it is first necessary to collect all Scripture passages on a certain subject, and then to try formulating the doctrine without the slightest contradiction.

She explains it as follows: "Make the Bible its own expositor, bringing together all that is said concerning a given subject at different times and under varied circumstances."[154] "Compare verse with verse, and you will find that Scripture is the key which unlocks Scripture."[155] One passage of Scripture will prove "a key to unlock other passages, and in this way light is shed upon the hidden meaning of the word, By comparing different texts treating the same subject, viewing their bearing on every side, the true meaning of the Scriptures will be made evident."[156]

This method began to be extensively used during the Protestant Reformation [157] and is still to be employed. She not only recommends this method of Bible study in a general way but recommends the use of this method to understand difficult passages.[158] It is the method on the basis of which the Bible student discovers the hidden or true meaning of the text,[159] to gain new insights,[160] to correct misinterpretations,[161] and to solve theological disagreements and perplexities among believers.[162]

---

153 "Notes of Travel."
154 "Search the Scriptures."
155 *Counsels to Teachers*, 437.
156 *Fundamentals of Education*, 187; cf. *Counsels to Teachers*, 437.
157 See e.g., *Great Controversy*. 203.
158 *Christian Education*, 59; *Steps to Christ*, 90-91.
159 *Fundamentals of Education*, 187; «Bible Study» *Signs of the Times*, Sept. 26, 1895.
160 See, *Testimonies*, 4:499.
161 MS 4, 1896 in *Manuscript Releases*, 4:56.
162 *Great Controversy*, 354, 423; cf. White, *Testimonies to Ministers*, 476.

Typology

The second approach again derived from Scripture is the typological method. It is intended to reveal the true meaning of the type and the fulfillment of its antitype. Ellen White fully endorses the typological method as legitimate in the formulation of doctrine.

Its importance she illustrates by the experience of Christ's disciples whose faith was founded on the testimony about Christ in "the types and prophecies of the Old Testament."[163] Christ the "originator" of the Jewish ceremonial system of worship of types and symbols designed it to teach "spiritual and heavenly things"[164] and important truths concerning the atonement."[165] Its ritual, pointing to "future redemption,"[166] represented the "gospel in symbol."[167] "Great truths" are revealed by this system which has as its "central object" to point people to "the Lamb of God that was to take away the sin of the world."[168] The scope of the typological method is immense for it pertains not only to Christ's sacrifice at the cross but also to His heavenly priesthood which lasts till the end of the world.[169]

Contextual Considerations

Ellen White approves of Miller's method that "every word must have its proper bearing on the subject presented in the Bible."[170] This means that each word of a particular subject must be in harmony with the context of the whole Bible.

She opposes the proof text method, which disregards the proper context, warning against the practice of some who "in order to sustain erroneous doctrines or unchristian practices" use certain "passages of Scripture separated from the context, perhaps quoting half of a single verse as proving their point, when the remaining portion would

---

163 *Desire of Ages*, 799.
164 *SDA Bible Commentary*, 7:933.
165 *Great Controversy*, 420.
166 *SDA Bible Commentary*, 6:1094.
167 *Prophet and Kings*, 489.
168 *Patriarchs and Prophets*, 594.
169 Ibid., 365; *Great Controversy*, 352.
170 "Notes of Travel."

show the meaning to be quite the opposite."[171] Her personal use of texts indicates that she has no objection against using a string of texts to proof a point provided they are in harmony with the whole Biblical context on the subject.

Lifestyle and Theology

Using proper methods in theology will not automatically guarantee sound theology, new truth, proper insights, concepts, or discoveries. The lifestyle of the theologians is crucial to the value and quality of their theology.

The successful outcome of correct methods of theology Ellen White links intimately with the spiritual condition of the interpreter. Correct theological discoveries, therefore, come only as the results of diligent and prayerful study of the Bible.

Persons engaged in the pursuit of theology, be they professionals or laity, must have a vital connection with Christ,[172] daily growing in grace,[173] and living a righteous life.[174] Their lifestyle has to be characterized by walking obediently in the present light,[175] including the light of health reform,[176] and involves purging sin from their lives.[177] Humility instead of pride should dominate their attitudes[178] and a willingness to accept and apply old truths.[179] Chosen and illuminated by the Holy Spirit,[180] they will constantly advance in proportion to the light[181] and recognize the Spirit of Prophecy as a continuing source of truth.[182]

---

171 *Great Controversy,* 521. cf. Judas' approach in White, *Desire of Ages,* 719.
172 *Writers and Editors,* 35; *Christ's Object Lessons,* 130-131.
173 *Testimonies,* 5:706.
174 *Writers and Editors,* 34,35.
175 *My Life Today,* 310. cf. *Testimonies,* 2:67.
176 Ibid., 67, 70-71.
177 *Ministry of Healing,* 464-465.
178 "Be Zealous and Repent," *Review and Herald,* December 23, 1890.
179 *Christ's Object Lessons,* 127; *Testimonies,* 5:369.
180 *Gospel Workers,* 297; "Be Zealous."
181 *Testimonies,* 5:534.
182 See, *Life Sketches,* 198-200.

When any of these lifestyle characteristics are absent there is no assurance that the result of their theological study is sound or can be trusted.

Finally, it is important to realize that it is a lifestyle of cherishing Christ's principles which is the determining element in the judgment.[183] "Those whom Christ commends in the Judgment, may have known little of theology, but they have cherished His principles. Through the influence of the divine Spirit they have been a blessing to those about them."[184] Among the saved will be persons who have had "no opportunity to understand the philosophy of theology"[185] as known in the popular theology of the world.

183 *Maranatha,* 320.
184 *Desire of Ages,* 638.
185 "Ye Did It To Me," *Signs of the Times, August 7,* 1893.

3

The Adventist Theologian, the Three Angels' Messages, and the Unity of the Church

This paper is written in the context of God's mandate to the Seventh-day Adventist Church. This mandate calls for Seventh-day Adventists to proclaim the great commission, focusing on the three angels' messages of Revelation 14. Toward the end of her life the prophetess to the remnant summarized this commission in the following words:

> In a special sense, Seventh-day Adventists have been set in the world as watchmen and light-bearers. To them has been entrusted the last warning for a perishing world. On them is shining wonderful light from the Word of God. They have been given a work of the most solemn import—the proclamation of the first, second, and third angels' messages. There is no other work of so great importance. They are to allow nothing else to absorb their attention.[1]

This mandate involves all church members, regardless of their occupations. All members have as their highest calling the responsibility to disseminate the three angels' messages—Christ's last message of mercy.

What does this mean for Adventist theologians? It means that they are privileged to participate in unitedly sharing these messages from their respective theological disciplines. No matter how demanding their disciplines might be, the overarching call for the theologians

---

Presented at the 2nd International Bible Conference Izmir, Turkey, July 7-18, 2006. Used with permission.

1   E. G. White, *Testimonies*, 9: 19 (1909)

is to join with church members in sharing Christ's last offer of salvation as the only hope of humanity to a dying world. Theologians also would assist in answering challenges and criticisms against our message and mission.

The effectiveness of our church's mission depends on the unity of how united theologians in executing this divine mandate of the three angels' messages, and their ability to serve the church and work together with its membership in implementing this mission.

Now the author will focus on the implications of the three angels' messages for Adventist theologians, the role they play in proclaiming these messages, and how they can contribute to the unity of the church.

Significance of the Three Angels' Messages

To obtain a clear understanding of the task of the Adventist theologian regarding the three angels' messages, we need define what we mean by these messages.[2]

From the outset, it is important to realize that interpretation of these messages did not happen by chance, guessing, or speculation. Primary sources show that Divine Providence guided our pioneers in the interpretation of these messages, firmly establishing the foundations of our faith. Through "earnest prayer and careful research of the Inspired Word"[3] they discovered that these messages reveal the truth that prepares men and women for Jesus' second coming.

After the Great Disappointment of 1844, Adventists, with fasting and praying, frequently met together, often until late at night—sometimes all night—searching the Scriptures to understand the mystery of their experience in the autumn of 1844, the Great Disappointment.[4]

---

2   For the historical theological development of the three angels' messages among the pioneers, see Gerard Damsteegt, *Foundations of the Seventh-day Adventist Message and Mission* (Grand Rapids, MI: Wm. B. Eerdmans, 1977). Since 1988 it has been reprinted by Andrews University Press, Berrien Springs, MI 49104.
3   White, "As You Have Received ... So Walk," *Review and Herald*, August 19, 1909.
4   Ibid., *Special Testimonies*, Series B, No. 2, 56, 57).

In a series of Bible Conferences from 1846 through 1848, during which the Holy Spirit manifested Himself in a very unique manner through the Spirit of Prophecy, the mandate for the message and mission of the remnant church was clearly formulated. In 1849, as a result of these conferences, Ellen White could say, "We have the truth. We know it."[5] Reflecting on this providential guidance, she later remarked, "the Lord would have us walk and work in perfect unity" for it is "in unity of spirit and action will be our strength."[6]

We will now view how Seventh-day Adventists have interpreted these messages since this guidance.

The First Angel's Message

The first angel's message proclaims the everlasting gospel message of the good news of salvation for the time of the end (Rev. 14:6). It reveals the good tidings of the mystery of God, that through the atoning sacrifice at Calvary, Jesus Christ has paid the penalty for our sins, redeemed us from the kingdom of Satan, and has adopted us as sons and daughters of God, giving us precious gift of eternal life which will be fully experienced at Christ's second coming.

Since 1844 the everlasting gospel has been calling people to repentance with a sense of urgency as never before. The call is made with a loud voice to every human being to fear God and give glory to Him. It is a call for a thorough repentance, demanding a surrender of all physical, mental, and spiritual powers to the Creator and Redeemer. It leads persons to have such a true fear of sin that they will no longer to continue the sinful lifestyles of the world.

The reason for the urgency of this call is that the hour of His judgment has arrived. This message calls people to repent because the final judgment has already begun. Since 1844 the heavenly records have been opened (Daniel 7:9-11), and the deeds of God's professed people are being investigated in the light of His eternal law, the standard of the judgment. From that time onward, the Scriptures direct our attention to the ark containing the Ten Commandments in the

5   Letter, E. G. White to the Hastingses, No. 18, January 11, 1850.
6   Ibid., "As You Have Received ... So Walk," *Review and Herald*, August 19, 1909.

Most Holy Place of His heavenly temple (Rev. 11:19) and the relevance of this law in the final judgment.

The first angel's call concludes with an invitation to worship God as the Creator. This brings out the significance of true worship, which is only accomplished through keeping the Sabbath holy. The second and third messages bring out the tragic consequences about those who reject the first angel's message and to continue to practice false worship forms.

The Second Angel's Message

The second angel's message (Rev. 14:8), explains the result of the rejection of the first angel's message. In the historicist time frame of prophecy, this refers to the rejection of the Great Second Advent movement and the persecution of Advent believers by the Protestant churches, especially in North America.

When during 1843 and 1844 the Adventists observed that the Protestant churches opposed the first angel's message and persecuted and excommunicated them from their churches, their attention was naturally drawn to the second angel's message that announced the fall of Babylon.

Using the historicist prophetic interpretation, many Protestants had interpreted the little horn of Daniel 7, the first beast of Revelation 13, and the harlot and Babylon of Relation 17 as the apostate Roman Catholic Church and the antichrist of Bible prophecy. When the Protestant churches rejected the Advent message of Daniel 8:14 about the cleansing of the sanctuary, Adventists limited the term "Babylon" no longer only to the Roman Catholic Church, but also the Protestant churches.

The Protestant churches, so highly favored by God during the Reformation, at this time "fell from the favor of God."[7] Now they, like the Roman Catholic Church, had become a part of Babylon, and joined the apostate spiritual confusion at the end of time. Adventists who

---

7   Ibid., *Early Writings*, 237.

left their churches or were disfellowshiped became a part of a unique movement, which they called the remnant church of prophecy.

The justification for being the prophetic remnant is based on the fact that Babylon had fallen and that the only hope for God's people was to come out of Babylon and join the remnant of the last days, who keep the commandments of Jesus and the faith of Jesus, and have the testimony of Jesus (Rev. 14:12; 12:17).

The fall of Babylon, therefore, became the biblical justification for the existence of the remnant church. If Babylon had not fallen there would have been hope for its religious organizations to revive and reform. But after their fall became a historical fact, God raised up the remnant church as a place of refuge for His people that they might find shelter from the coming destruction brought about by the seven last plagues when they hear the call, "Come out of her My people," (Rev. 18:4).

The Third Angel's Message

The third angel's message (Rev. 14:9-12) proclaims with a loud cry the last warning to an apostate world to escape the final wrath that God will pour out upon all the disobedient. It contains the most severe warning ever given to humanity against worshiping the beast and his image. It points to the outpouring of the seven last plagues that follow the close of probation, when there is no more mercy because Christ has completed His intercessory ministry in the heavenly sanctuary. God's judgments upon the human race have always been mixed with mercy; the judgments under the last plagues follow the close of probation after which there is no more mercy.

In the seven last plagues, God's wrath falls upon humanity without any mercy because of His indignation against a rebellious world that was willing to utterly annihilate His remnant. The angel said, "You are righteous, O Lord, the One who is and who was and who is to be, because You have judged these things. For they have shed the blood of saints and prophets, and You have given them blood to drink. For it is their just due." (Rev. 16:5, 6).

In the context of historicist interpretation of Revelation 13, the first beast represents Roman Catholicism; the image of the beast, apostate Protestantism. The first power has enforced false worship on the world through most of the Christian era; apostate Protestantism will participate in this effort in the very near future, which will be seen in an enforcement of Sunday as the day to worship God on a worldwide scale.

When Sunday worship will be forced on people the final scenes of Revelation 13 will transpire. Those who bow to the pressure and worship according to the laws enacted through the influence of both of these powers will receive a mark on their foreheads or on their hands. Consequently, they will be subject to the seven last plagues and will utterly perish.

Just before Christ's return all non-Christian religions will unite with this apostate Christian coalition against the Remnant Church. At that time Babylon will be a three-fold union, composed of Catholicism, apostate Protestantism, and spiritualism that embraces all other religions, to influence humanity to accept Sunday worshi Under the seventh plague this three-fold apostate union of Babylon will fall apart and perish (Rev. 16:19).

However, before Christ has completed the investigative judgment, the Remnant will give one final invitation to accept God's mercy—the loud cry of the third angel's message (Rev. 18:1). It is this final and greatest outpouring of the Holy Spirit—the latter rain, that brings about this cry. This is the last and greatest revival and reformation in the history of humanity and also the last invitation of mercy to the world. Those who join this remnant movement receive the seal of the living God from the sealing angel (Rev. 7:1-4) and will be saved from the coming full wrath of God manifested in the seven last plagues (Rev. 15, 16).

Unity in Interpreting the Three Angels' Messages

The above explanation of the three angels' messages is based on the historicist hermeneutic of apocalyptic prophecy. For the Seventh-day Adventist church to fulfill its divine mandate, it is absolutely necessary that theologians be united with the rest of the church's membership in the interpretation of the meaning of these messages. If theologians do not fully accept the historicist method of prophetic interpretation, their influence brings confusion and disunity to the mission of the church and will seriously delay the finishing of the work of preparing people for Christ's return.

From the beginning of the movement, Seventh-day Adventists have followed the historicist prophetic hermeneutic, which has its roots in the early church and was widely practiced during the Protestant Reformation. It was formulated by William Miller, adopted by our pioneers, and confirmed by the Spirit of Prophecy. The success of Adventism stands and falls with this hermeneutic.

Ellen White clearly endorsed Miller's hermeneutic. She stated:

Those who are engaged in proclaiming the third angel's message[8] are searching the Scriptures upon the same plan that Father Miller adopted. In the little book entitled 'Views of the Prophecies and Prophetic Chronology,' Father Miller gives the following simple but intelligent and important rules for Bible study and interpretation:

"1. Every word must have its proper bearing on the subject presented in the Bible;

2. All Scripture is necessary, and may be understood by diligent application and study;

3. Nothing revealed in Scripture can or will be hid from those who ask in faith, not wavering;

4. To understand doctrine, bring all the scriptures together on the subject you wish to know, then let every word have its proper influence; and if you can form your theory without a contradiction, you cannot be in error;

5. Scripture must be its own expositor, since it is a rule of itself. If I depend on a teacher to expound to me, and he should guess at its meaning, or desire to have it so on ac-

---

8   When Ellen White mentions the phrase "third angel's message", she does not confine it to Rev. 14:9-12 but the includes all three angel's messages of Rev. 14:6-12. See *Spiritual Gifts*, 1:171 and Damsteegt, *Foundations*, 241, 242.

count of his sectarian creed, or to be thought wise, then his guessing, desire, creed, or wisdom is my rule, and not the Bible."

The above is a portion of these rules; and in our study of the Bible we shall all do well to heed the principles set forth.[9]

Let us examine these hermeneutical guidelines.

The first rule that "every word must have its proper bearing on the subject presented in the Bible" stresses the importance that each word of a particular subject must be in harmony with the context of the whole Bible. This contextual method of interpreting the Scriptures guards against taking texts out of their proper context.

In this light, Ellen White warned against the practice of some, who, "in order to sustain erroneous doctrines or unchristian practices," use certain "passages of Scripture separated from the context, perhaps quoting half of a single verse as proving their point, when the remaining portion would show the meaning to be quite the opposite."[10] Her personal use of texts indicates that she has no objection against using a string of texts to prove a point, provided they are in harmony with the whole Biblical context on the subject as Miller suggested.

The second rule that "all Scripture is necessary, and may be understood by diligent application and study" stresses the importance of the larger context. Before interpreters come to a conclusion, they need to consult the whole Bible to ascertain that the interpretation of a passage or text is in complete harmony with its immediate as well as the larger context of the Bible. It points out that the whole biblical canon should be the context in which the interpreter operates. In this light, Ellen White pointed out that one "should learn to view the Word as a whole, and to see the relation of its parts."[11]

This rule cautions us against the practice of using a canon within a canon that draws conclusions from a narrow approach by limiting

9   White, "Notes of Travel," *Review and Herald,* November 25, 1884.
10   Ibid., *Great Controversy,* 521. cf. White, *Desire of Ages,* 719.
11   Ibid., *Education,* 190.

research to a particular passage, chapter, book or section of the Bible which is done often in the name of exegesis.

The third rule that "nothing revealed in Scripture can or will be hid from those who ask in faith, not wavering" has as its purpose to inspire interpreters with confidence that, when they ask God in faith in their study of the Bible, He will make plain to them what He has revealed.

The fourth rule that "to understand doctrine, bring all the scriptures together on the subject you wish to know, then let every word have its proper influence; and if you can form your theory without a contradiction, you cannot be in error" has been described as the analogy of Scripture method or Scripture principle.

This method teaches that to understand Bible doctrine correctly, it is first necessary to collect all Scripture passages on a certain subject and then to try formulating the doctrine without the slightest contradiction. The method of comparing Scripture with Scripture was also extensively used during the Protestant Reformation.[12]

Commenting on this rule, Ellen White explained that in the study of the Scriptures there is the need of "bringing together all that is said concerning a given subject at different times and under varied circumstances."[13] "Compare verse with verse, and you will find that Scripture is the key which unlocks Scripture."[14] One passage of Scripture will prove "a key to unlock other passages, and in this way light is shed upon the hidden meaning of the word. By comparing different texts treating the same subject, viewing their bearing on every side, the true meaning of the Scriptures will be made evident."[15]

She especially recommends the use of this method to understand difficult passages,[16] to discover the hidden or true meaning of the tex-

---

12   See e.g. Ibid., *Great Controversy.* 203.

13   Ibid., "Search the Scriptures" *Review and Herald,* October 9, 1883.

14   Ibid., *Counsels to Teachers,* 437.

15   Ibid., *Fundamentals of Education,* 187; cf. White, *Counsels to Teachers,* 437.

16   Ibid., Christian Education, 59; White, *Steps to Christ,* 90, 91.

t,[17]to gain new insights,[18] to correct misinterpretations,[19] and to solve theological disagreements and perplexities among believers.[20]

The fifth rule that "Scripture must be its own expositor, since it is a rule of itself" means that the Bible itself is the key to understand the Bible. In the interpretation of Scripture, therefore, it is not necessary to depend on extra biblical sources or commentators.

On this very point White explained, "we are not to accept the opinions of commentators as the voice of God" because "they were erring mortals like ourselves. God has given reasoning powers to us as well as to them. We should make the Bible its own expositor."[21] She places the use of this method within the broad perspective of Christ's role in the great controversy between good and evil.[22] Methods of interpretation, therefore, must be derived from the Bible.

Theologians to Uphold the *Sola Scriptura* Principle

In light of the general departure from Bible truth, Ellen White stresses the "need of a return to the great Protestant principle—the Bible, and the Bible only, as the rule of faith and duty."[23] In regard to the crucial question, "How Should We Then Live?" the answer is to be found in the Bible only—the *Sola Scriptura* principle. Here the answers to the question challenging humans, "What Must I Do to Inherit Eternal Life?" are plainly revealed.

No extra biblical literature is necessary. All questions regarding how human beings can be saved and how they can obtain atonement for their sins are spelled out in the Bible. She states, "Searching the Scriptures alone will bring the knowledge of the true God and Jesus Christ whom He has sent."[24]

---

17   Ibid., *Fundamentals of Education*, 187; Ibid., "Bible Study" *Signs of the Times*, Sept. 26, 1895.
18   See Ibid., *Testimonies*, 4:499.
19   Ibid., MS 4, 1896 in *Manuscript Releases*, 4:56.
20   Ibid., *Great Controversy*, 354, 423; cf. Ibid., *Testimonies to Ministers*, 476.
21   Ibid., *Testimonies to Ministers*, 106.
22   See Ibid., *Education*, 190.
23   Ibid., *Great Controversy*, 204, 205.
24   Ibid., *Fundamentals of Education*, 415.

Adventist theologians need to keep in mind that in the quest for truth, therefore, there is no need to study extra-Biblical sources to arrive at the ultimate truth of how to be saved. The divine revelation in the Scriptures is fully adequate. "All that man needs to know and can know of God," she says, "has been revealed in His Word and in the life of His Son, the great Teacher."[25]

Theologians and the Spirit of Prophecy

In the light of "the Bible and the Bible only" principle Adventist theologians have wrestled with the role of the writings of Ellen White in the interpretation of the Scriptures. Here the Bible itself provides the answer. The Bible informs its readers that during the time of the end the testimony of Jesus through the Spirit of Prophecy will be present among the prophetic remnant (Rev 12:17; 19:10; 22:9).

The Bible, Ellen White writes, assures true believers of continual guidance by the Holy Spirit. God has promised to give "visions in the 'last days;' not for a new rule of faith, but for the comfort of His people, and to correct those who err from Bible truth."[26]The reason for this special manifestation of the Holy Spirit in the end-time is because "little heed is given to the Bible." Through the Spirit of Prophecy "the Lord has given a lesser light to lead men and women to the greater light."[27] Ellen White makes the following comparison: "In ancient times God spoke to men by the mouth of prophets and apostles. In these days He speaks to them by the testimonies of His Spirit."[28]

If theologians believe that today God especially speaks to the remnant, it is of paramount importance to listen to the testimonies of His Spirit and find out what are God's messages and counsel for the end-time generation. To consult this source of revelation is not contrary to the Bible, but in full harmony with its counsels.

---

25 Ibid., MS 124, 1903 in *Bible Commentary*, 6:1079.
26 Ibid., *Early Writings*, 78.
27 Ibid., "An Open Letter...," *Review and Herald*, January 20, 1903.
28 Ibid., *Testimonies*, 5:661. Italics supplied.

Theologians and the Testimonies

What is the relation of Ellen White's messages or testimonies to the Bible? It is important that theologians realize that her writings are not an addition to the Bible, but an aid to its understanding. "God," she said, "has seen fit in this manner to bring the minds of His people to His word, to give them a clearer understanding of it."[29] They are not to give "new light" but "to impress vividly upon the heart the truths of inspiration already revealed." She emphasizes that "additional truth is not brought out; but God has through the Testimonies simplified the great truths already given and in His own chosen way brought them before the people to awaken and impress the mind with them, that all may be left without excuse."[30]

Although these testimonies are not new light, they contain light that corrects errors and defines truth: "The Lord has given me much light that I want the people to have; for there is instruction that the Lord has given me for His people." She adds, "this is now to come before the people, because it has been given to correct specious errors and to specify what is truth."[31] Theologians, therefore, need to consult these messages and see how they can assist to discover the deeper meaning of the Scriptures and avoid incorrect interpretations.

The establishment of the foundations of the Seventh-day Advent Church shows the intimate relationship between the Bible and the Spirit of Prophecy. Often Ellen White's visions would confirm the results of the Bible studies of the Adventist Sabbath keepers during the formative years of the remnant. There were times when the Bible conferences were stalled and her visions broke the deadlock, guiding the believers to the correct Biblical solution.

The truth—"especially concerning the ministration of Christ in the heavenly sanctuary, and the message of Heaven for these last days, as given by the angels of the fourteenth chapter of Revelation," she says, "has been sought out by prayerful study, and testified to by the miracle-working power of the Lord." It is God Himself, she declares,

---

29   Ibid., 663.
30   Ibid., 665.
31   Ibid., Letter 127, 1910 in *Selected Messages*, 3:32. The published source has a typographical error. It refers to Letter 117 instead of 127.

who "through His Word and the testimony of His Spirit" has revealed the permanence of these "fundamental principles [way marks or land marks] that are based upon unquestionable authority."[32]

The Meaning of the "Bible Only"

An analysis of Ellen White's use of the phrase "the Bible and the Bible only" reveals that she contrasts it with human "views and ideas,"[33] erroneous traditions on the Sabbath and the Law of God,[34] opinions of scholars, scientists, theologians,"[35] "sayings and doings of men,"[36] "human wisdom,"[37] false visions,[38] views of the churches steeped in popular theology from which the early Adventists separated themselves,[39] the "religions of fable and tradition," "imaginary religion," "a religion of words and forms," and "tradition and human theories and maxims."[40] These phrases show that she uses the "Bible only" to contrast Biblical truth with the unbiblical positions of religious traditions.

This expression "the Bible only" she never used for contrasting her own writings with the Bible. In Ellen White's mind there was perfect harmony between the Bible and her writings because "the Holy Ghost is the author of the Scriptures and the author of the spirit of prophecy."[41] Therefore "it is impossible that the teachings of the Spirit should ever be contrary to that of the word."[42]

This unique relationship between the Bible and the Spirit of Prophecy has given the latter a place above all extra-Biblical sources. Consequently in Bible study the writings of the Spirit of Prophecy hold a superior position over other research tools.

32 Ibid., *Selected Messages,* 1:208.
33 Ibid., "Missionary Appeal."
34 Ibid., *Great Controversy,* 448.
35 Ibid. 595.
36 Ibid., *Counsels on Sabbath Work,* 84.
37 Ibid., *Fundamentals of Education,* 200.
38 Ibid., *Selected Messages,* 2:85.
39 Ibid., *Writers and Editors,* 145.
40 Ibid., *Prophets and Kings,* 624-626.
41 Ibid., Letter 92, 1900.
42 Ibid., *Great Controversy,* vii.

Theologians to Preserve Church Unity

Theologians have a serious obligation to see that their influence will preserve the unity of the church by upholding its end-time message and mission. They do well to remember Ellen White's comment in this regard: "Those who have accepted the truth of the third angel's message are to hold it fast by faith, and it will hold them from drifting into superstitions and theories that would separate them from one another and from God."[43]

When she mentions the "third angel's message" she does not see it apart from the first and second angel's messages, but includes it in this phrase all three angels' messages. To understand and accept the third angel's message necessitates the acceptance of the first and second angels' messages. Only then the third angel's message could be comprehended.[44]

Theologians are to uphold the gospel proclamation for the end-time, which is the key to the moral restoration of humanity. White emphasized, "A great work is to be accomplished in setting before men the saving truths of the gospel."[45] In spelling out the far-reaching effect of these gospel truths, she stated, "This is the means ordained by God to stem the tide of moral corruption. This is His means of restoring His moral image in man. It is His remedy for universal disorganization. It is the power that draws men together in unity. To present these truths is the work of the third angel's message."[46] This is not one mission amongst others. No. "The Lord designs that the presentation of this message shall be the highest, greatest work carried on in the world at this time."[47]

As servants of the church, theologians need to understand the depth, height, and width of the last message of mercy that unites Seventh-day Adventists so that they become aware of significant neglected aspects of this all-embracing message. An important task is to impress the church's leadership and

---

43   Ibid., *Heavenly Places,* 349
44   Ibid., *Spiritual Gifts,* 1:171. See Damsteegt, *Foundations,* 242.
45   White, *Testimonies,* 1:11.
46   Ibid.
47   Ibid.

laity that in our mission to restore humanity in the image of God is to make sure that health reform is to stand out more prominently in the proclamation of the third angel's message. The principles of health reform are found in the word of God. The gospel of health is to be firmly linked with the ministry of the word. It is the Lord's design that the restoring influence of health reform shall be a part of the last great effort to proclaim the gospel message.[48]

Theologians ought to be a part of the mission outreach of the church, working together with evangelists and medical missionaries, supporting them in the proclamation of the three angels' messages. Stressing the need for unity in action, White appealed for "the necessity of all our laborers working in unity, with one mind and one judgment."[49]

The Role of the Holy Spirit

The unity among theologians is not something they bring about by themselves in professional societies, committees, conventions, or conferences. Unity is brought about as a result of genuine conversion and the Holy Spirit; division is caused by the absence of conversion and the Spirit. "All who are truly converted unto the proclamation of the third angel's message," White wrote, "must not present to the world, to angels, and to men, division in the place of unity. The truth of God sanctifies the receiver to be a channel and representative of His grace to the world and to angels and to men. All who are called [are] prepared and aided by one Agency."[50]

It is the Holy Spirit who brings theologians into an intimate unity of brotherly love, fellowship, and cooperation, as well as giving their full support to the Church. "From one great and powerful Source there would be love and unity; their Christian instrumentality to be proved and to glorify God in love and harmonious action, each strengthening the other and each taking diligent heed to his own course

---

48   Ibid., *Testimony Studies on Diet and Foods,* 88.
49   Ibid., "Our Responsibility as Stewards," *Home Missionary,* December 1, 1894.
50   Ibid., "Each Follower of Christ is Called to Work; All are to Copy Christ, the Pattern; Harmony to Prevail," Ms 130, 1901 in 16MR 196

of action in the great and solemn work before them in presenting the sanctifying truth to souls ready to die."[51]

The achievement of unity in the church does not come easily. A clear stand must be taken against falsehood and heresies. White stated, "Evil must be assailed; falsehood and error must be made to appear in their true character; sin must be denounced; and the testimony of every believer in the truth must be as one. All your little differences, which arouse the combative spirit among brethren, are devices of Satan to divert minds from the great and fearful issue before us."[52]

True unity that brings genuine peace will not exist when a false peace reigns in the church. White pointed out that we need to make a united effort against falsehoods that presently exist: "The true peace will come among God's people when through united zeal and earnest prayer the false peace that exists to a large degree is disturbed. Now there is earnest work to do. Now is the time to manifest your soldierly qualities; let the Lord's people present a united front to the foes of God and truth and righteousness."[53]

Referring to how the early Christians experienced unity, White said, "when the Holy Spirit was poured out upon the early church, 'the whole multitude of them that believed were of one heart and of one soul.' The Spirit of Christ made them one. This is the fruit of abiding in Christ."[54]

Describing the process by which the Holy Sprit tries to bring about this desired unity today, she said,

> We have need of divine illumination. Every individual is striving to become a center of influence; and until God works for His people, they will not see that subordination to God is the only safety for any soul. His transforming grace upon human hearts will lead to unity that has not yet been realized; for all

---

51　Ibid., 16MR 196.
52　Ibid., MR311, 48
53　Ibid.
54　Ibid.

who are assimilated to Christ will be in harmony with one another. The Holy Spirit will create unity.[55]

Unity and Diversity Among Theologians

Throughout the years the writings of Seventh-day Adventist theologians have increasingly come under scrutiny by its membershi Internet communications reveal a growing number of controversies in the remnant church. This is unfortunate, for it negatively affects the mission thrust of the remnant church. Several factors are responsible for these controversies that are causing divisions amongst Seventh-day Adventists. From the above, it is clear that theologians need a unity based on Christ's last message of mercy.

One major factor may be a misunderstanding of academic freedom and the often- claimed argument that we have in our church unity in diversity, not uniformity. Again it will be helpful to consider the counsels of the Spirit of Prophecy on how to unitedly publish about our unique message.

Ellen White strongly encouraged writing on this subject but to keep in mind the nature of unity in diversity. She compares this unity to the relationship between the organs of the human body. Said she, "In regard to our brethren writing on the third angel's message. Let them write. Bear in mind that in the branches of the vine there is diversity in unity... There is an unseen, conscious, indivisible unity, keeping the bodily machinery in action, each part working in harmony with every other... "[56]

She cautions against uniformity, stating, "we are not to feel that we must speak the very same things, giving the same representation in the same words, and yet there is to be unity in the diversity."[57] She illustrates a healthy diversity by pointing to the gospels, explaining, "all the different testimonies unite to form one whole, as the books of the Bible are brought together, and bound under one cover. But

---

55   Letter 25b, 1892 (MR311, 48)
56   Ibid., Letter 53, 1900, 1-7. (To S. N. Haskell, April 5, 1900.) "Diversity in Unity in God's Work," MR 550, in 8MR 66.
57   Ibid., 67

should Matthew, Mark, Luke and John go off on some tangent, contradicting each other's testimony, then there would be confusion. In all the presentation of truth by different minds, there is to be unity in diversity."[58]

She warns against the desire of trying to be different, stating, "one must not labor to have everything that comes from his mind entirely different from that which comes from another man's mind."[59] Instead of attempting to be different, she calls on the need to follow the leadings of the Holy Spirit. Said she, "he is to follow in the line where the Spirit of the Lord shall direct, then there will be different figures and different ways of presentation, that will interest and educate different minds."[60]

Striving for originality is also dangerous. Said White.

Some are always straining to get something original; this places them in great danger. They produce something new, that is not according to the Word of God, and they have not the discernment to see the real harm that results from their ambition to excel some other one in new and strange productions. Thus error comes to appear to them as truth, and they present it as wonderful new light, when it is an innovation that makes of none effect a 'Thus saith the Lord.'[61]

White emphasized the need to leave room for the workings of the Holy Spirit. "Let all be under the controlling influence of the Holy Spirit of God. Under the direction of the Holy Spirit, one may use the same expressions used by a fellow-worker under the same guidance. He should not make an effort to do this, nor not to do it, but leave the mind to be acted upon by the Holy Spirit. There is one thing all should do, 'Endeavor to keep the Unity of the Spirit, in the bonds of peace.'"[62]

She cautions those writing on the truth against selfishness in their evaluation of others who do not express truths in the exactly the sa-

---

58   Ibid.
59   Ibid.
60   Ibid.
61   Ibid.
62   Ibid.

me way: "Men may not have precisely the same way of viewing or expressing truths as we have, yet they may be just as precious in the sight of God as we are. There is not to be a thread of selfishness or self-exaltation in our work, for we are drawing our spiritual supplies from the same store-house, and are wholly and entirely dependent upon God, for His grace and His Spirit's working."[63]

Threats to Theological Unity in the Church

Use of Extra Biblical Scholarly Sources

In reflecting on present influences that endanger the unity among theologians, the author can see no greater danger for the church than the adoption of non-Adventist theological views in the interpretation and exposition of Scripture and its prophecies.

Light from the heavenly sanctuary revealed that since 1844 Adventists are living in the most solemn era of earth's history when Christ our High Priest is completing His investigative judgment. The Holy Spirit is also purifying the Remnant Church in preparation for the final sealing of His people that protects them from the coming calamities. Through these new insights Adventists have been motivated to adopt a special end-time lifestyle in preparation for the second advent. This understanding is totally absent among non-Adventists. When Seventh-day Adventist scholars evaluated these end-time lifestyle practices in the light of non-Adventist sources, the result has been heated controversies without end, seriously dividing our churches.

All Seventh-day Adventist scholars are no longer careful in scrutinizing whether the non-Adventist sources and even the Adventist sources they quote are using the same hermeneutics that Seventh-day Adventists have applied since the pioneers. Before using any source into our research and writing the question needs to be asked, "Do these authors approach the Bible with the same high view of Scripture, have the same concepts on revelation and inspiration, the nature and infallibility of Scripture, and the 'Bible only' principle?" This is of paramount importance. Differences on these vital concepts affect the correct interpretation of the biblical text.

---

63   Ibid., 68.

How many Seventh-day Adventist scholars consider impact of the fall of Babylon on the theological disciplines of these churches since 1844? It is important to remember that following 1844, the churches gradually departed from the historicist method of interpretation of the Bible and a spiritual darkness came upon them that impacted them in areas of prophetic interpretation, theology, and lifestyle. In their departure from historicism, the churches gave up the sound methods used by the Protestant Reformers and early Adventists, leading them into futurism, preterism, idealism and other speculative approaches. These views have significantly influenced the scholarly community in their interpretation of the Bible with its subsequent sad results.

The prophet to the remnant noted the dangers of the so-called "popular theology" in these fallen churches. The nature of this theology is speculative and is characterized by incorrect interpretations of Scripture. It exalts human theories above the Word of God and stands in sharp contrast to the eternal truths taught by the Bible writers.[64] The presence of this theology is widespread. "To a large degree," Ellen White warned, "theology, as studied and taught, is but a record of human speculation."[65]

The problem with an erroneous speculative theology is that it has a detrimental effect on the on mind and judgment which exposes believers to temptations. The study of these speculations darkens the mind.[66] Ellen White said, it "perverts the judgment and opens the door to temptation, and through its influence Satan seeks to turn hearts from the truth." Its influence is directed to lowering the standards of Christian living.[67] It certainly does not prepare believers for the second advent. As an antidote, she recommends "an intelligent love for the truth" which "sanctifies the receiver, and keeps him from the enemy's deceptive snares.[68]

Unsound theology, Ellen White pointed out, confuses the intellect and disqualifies a person for teaching. As an example she mentioned

---

64   Ibid., *Great Controversy,* 126. See also Ibid., "Luther at Wittenberg," *Signs of the Times,* June 7, 1883.
65   Ibid., *Counsels to Teachers,* 380.
66   Ibid.
67   Ibid., 5MR 380. This view was the result of the theology of Dr. Jackson.
68   Ibid., "The Christian Pathway," *Signs of the Times,* March 6, 1884.

Dr. John H. Kellogg. Speaking of him, she says, his "theology is not sound; his mind is confused, and unless he sees his danger, his foundation will be swept away when the test comes. Unless he sees his danger and makes a decided change, he can not be endorsed as a safe, all-round teacher."[69]

Regarding this kind of theology, Ellen White perceived two dangers. One danger is a "scientific theology" which had been introduced into the Battle Creek church in 1906. Its impact leads people away from a true faith in God and raised questions about her writings.[70] As a result even prominent church leaders like the General Conference President A. G. Daniells and theologian W. C Prescott became confused about Ellen White's work, considering it a mystery.[71]

Ellen White wrote of a scene in which both Prescott and Daniells were conversing with Dr. Kellogg, listening to subtle reasoning prompted by the evil angels close by. She described the experience of these men as a life and death struggle because Dr. Kellogg's influence was so powerful that his subtle reasoning almost overwhelmed them.[72]

It was through an intervention of Providence that these men saw again the light. "Through the agency of a heavenly messenger, the thought came to the men to 'review the past experiences of the people of God; review the history of the work from the first,' and the question was asked, 'Has this work been what it has been represented to you to be?'" Next, "the heavenly messenger revealed to them 'scene after scene' until they saw truth bearing the signature of the heavenly in the past, then present, and still more decidedly in the future."[73]

The second danger of this theology is the work of higher criticism, later called biblical or historical criticism. This approach she characterizes as "dissecting, conjecturing, reconstructing" the Scriptures.[74]

---

69 Ibid., *Battle Creek Letters,* 87.

70 Ibid., "Hold Fast the Beginning of Your Confidence," *Review and Herald,* August 9, 1906. See *The Paulson Collection of Ellen G. White Letters,* 66; Ibid., MS 61, June 3, 1906.

71 Ibid. 10MR 333.

72 Ibid.

73 Ibid., 333, 334.

74 Ibid., *Education,* 227.

She considered it to be one of Satan's tools of deception. Through its "pleasing sentiments," she says, "the enemy of righteousness is seeking to lead souls into forbidden paths."[75]

The reason for her strong opposition to higher criticism is that it "is destroying faith in the Bible as a divine revelation; it is robbing God's word of power to control, uplift, and inspire human lives."[76] She compares its influence to the destructive effect of tradition and Rabbinical teaching in Christ's days.[77]

In a sermon she ironically contrasts the higher critics, whom she identifies as "poor, finite man on probation," with the true Higher Critic, "the Lord God of the universe who has spread the canopy of the heavens above us, and has made the stars and called them forth in their order."[78]

The Place of Extra Biblical Writings

The question theologians have to ponder is this, "How valuable are non-Seventh-day Adventist sources?"

As to the value of extra-biblical sources on Bible teachings, Ellen White says, "the opinions of learned men, the deductions of science, the creeds or decisions of ecclesiastical councils, as numerous and discordant as are the churches which they represent, the voice of the majority,—not one nor all of these should be regarded as evidence for or against any point of religious faith."[79]

On the value of commentaries she remarks, "many think that they must consult commentaries on the Scriptures in order to understand the meaning of the word of God." She does not object to their use, stating, "We would not take the position that commentaries should not be studied," but cautions that "it will take much discernment to discover the truth of God under the mass of the words of men."[80] She

---

75   Ibid., *Acts of the Apostles,* 474. His other tools are "evolution, spiritualism, theosophy, and pantheism (Ibid.).

76   Ibid., *Education,* 227.

77   Ibid., *Ministry of Healing,* 142.

78   Ibid., MS 43a, 1894.

79   Ibid., *Great Controversy,* 595.

80   Ibid., *Fundamentals of Education,* 187, 188.

says, "many think it essential to acquire an extensive knowledge of historical and theological writings" because "they suppose that this knowledge will be an aid to them in teaching the gospel" but "their laborious study of the opinions of men tends to the enfeebling of their ministry, rather than to its strengthening."[81]

There are, however, some areas of extra biblical sources Ellen White recommends studying. One area pertains to the investigation of the vast amount of truths God has given to His people throughout the past centuries. "The infinite treasures of truth have been accumulating from age to age. No representation could adequately impress us with the extent, the richness, of these vast resources. They are awaiting the demand of those who appreciate them."[82]

The purpose of such a study is to communicate God's truths to others. Said she, "these gems of truth are to be gathered up by God's remnant people, to be given by them to the world."[83]

Here she sees this study as a way to share with others the truths God has already given to past generations, but that have been lost over time. In the context of the second angel's message, she seemed especially to recommend a study of truths in non-biblical sources that were produced prior to the fall of Babylon in 1844 when there was not yet a general departure from the historicist hermeneutics.

Instead of studying the latest theological works and papers by scholars who do not employ the historicist hermeneutics in their productions, Seventh-day Adventist theologians should focus on discovering the gems of truth of the past that are still relevant in conveying the present truth today. This has an excellent potential for building bridges with non-Adventists Christians who have departed from the light of the Reformation by calling them back to the great foundational truths of the Scripture and its prophetic interpretation.

Unfortunately many Seventh-day Adventists have not followed this advice. Consequently, they have missed an important opportunity to discover these infinite treasures of truth. Commenting on the

---

81   Ibid., *Ministry of Healing*, 441.
82   Ibid., "An Appeal to Our Churches," *Review and Herald*, December 23, 1890.
83   Ibid.

reason of our failure, White observed, "self confidence and the obduracy of soul refuse the blessed treasure."[84]

It is therefore important for Seventh-day Adventist theologians to remember their place and function in the history of salvation. "God's workers today constitute the connecting link between the former workers, the church of history, and the church that is to be called out from the world and prepared to meet their Lord... From age to age the light which God has for the world has been imparted to the church militant."[85]

With this in mind, theologians need to highly respect the light of the past. "All the excellencies that have come through the belief of the truth from past ages to the present time, are to be treated with the utmost respect"[86]

Another area of extra-biblical sources is that of the study of sacred history which reveals the history of Bible prophecy. Said she, "Sacred history was one of the studies in the schools of the prophets. In the record of His dealings with the nations were traced the footsteps of Jehovah. So today we are to consider the dealings of God with the nations of the earth."[87] She challenged Bible interpreters to study prophetic history, stating "We are to see in history the fulfillment of prophecy, to study the workings of Providence in the great reformatory movements, and to understand the progress of events in the marshaling of the nations for the final conflict of the great controversy."[88]

This approach has great benefits, she explained: "Such study will give broad, comprehensive views of life. It will help us to understand something of its relations and dependencies, how wonderfully we are bound together in the great brotherhood of society and nations, and to how great an extent the oppression and degradation of one member means loss to all."[89] White had little appreciation of the study of history as it is commonly studied because it is concerned with man's

---

84   Ibid.
85   Ibid., *Special Testimonies,* Series A, No. 7. 1897, 11.
86   Ibid.
87   Ibid., *Counsels to Parents, Teachers, and Students,* 379.
88   Ibid., 379, 380.
89   Ibid.

achievements while "God's agency in the affairs of men is lost sight of. Few study the working out of His purpose in the rise and fall of nations."[90]

From the above, it seems clear that theologians should be very careful with the use of extra biblical sources. If these sources are in harmony with the biblical text they may be used, but if they are contrary to the obvious and clear literal reading of the text, they should be discarded. In no way should they be the key to determine the meaning of a biblical text or passage.

Those familiar with primary sources understand the conflicting views these sources frequently present. What are the criteria for theologians? Throughout their history Seventh-day Adventists have accepted views or data that were in harmony with the clear reading of the biblical text, but have discarded interpretations that were in conflict with the natural and obvious reading of the text. Theologians do well to follow this practice, remembering the impact of the events of 1844 and its subsequent light received by the remnant and the resulting darkness and confusion that developed as result of the rejection of truth.

The same is true of the need among theologians to understand the place of the writings of Ellen White in the quest of the truth of the Bible. There is a special blessing connected with understanding the significance of these writings for the unity and protection of the church. She said, "Men may get up scheme after scheme and the enemy will seek to seduce souls from the truth, but all who believe that the Lord has spoken though Sister White and has given her a message will be safe from the many delusions that will come in these last days."[91]

Theologians do well to keep this in mind.

Urgency of Unity in Our Message and Mission

More than one hundred years ago, Ellen White informed Seventh-day Adventists that the moment had arrived for the three angels'

90 Ibid.
91 Ibid., *Selected Messages,* 3:83, 84.

messages to swell into a loud cry. She said, "the time has come when the whole earth is to be enlightened with the glory of the angel which came down from heaven"[92] (Rev. 18:1). What has happened since that time? Have they progressed or regressed?

Towards the end of her life, she sadly explained why this event did not happen at that time, saying, "We may have to remain here in this world because of insubordination many more years, as did the children of Israel; but for Christ's sake, His people should not add sin to sin by charging God with the consequence of their own wrong course of action.[93]

It is clear that Seventh-day Adventists are involved in a tremendous warfare between the armies of Christ and those of Satan. Satan has been successful in muting the cry of the third angel and weakening their understanding of their identity and mission as God's prophetic remnant to prepare people for Jesus' coming so they will be able stand in the Day of the Lord. To remedy the situation, Adventists need to experience a great revival and reformation. To bring this about theologians may do well to heed the exhortation of the prophetic voice:

> Our success depends upon our unity. Our efficiency and the power of our influence depends upon our wise and unreserved cooperation with one another and with God. We are to advance the work in new territories, sustaining pure principles at every ste We are to cooperate with the angel that is flying in the midst of heaven [Rev. 14:9-11], who also is in harmony with the two former angels [Rev. 14:6-8] in forwarding the solemn event of the second appearing of Christ in the clouds of heaven with power and great glory.[94]

To bring this unity in the message and mission among Seventh-day Adventists about, theologians can play a crucial role if they are committed to work together with administrators, evangelists, and ministers, elders and lay persons.

---

92   Ibid., Manuscript 177, 1899 in MR 311, 48.
93   Ibid., Letter 184, 1901 (*Evangelism,* 696.
94   Ibid., Manuscript 177, 1899 in MR 311, 47.

Conclusion

Seventh-day Adventist theologians have a vital responsibility in the proclamation of the three angels' messages—the last message of mercy to a perishing world. In this task they need to cooperate closely with administrators, ministers, pastors, local elders, and lay persons.

Theologians need to be united on the message and mission as revealed through divine providence and guided by the historicist hermeneutics of the Advent pioneers. This message is based on the Sola Scriptura principle and the affirmation of the Spirit of Prophecy as manifested in the writings of Ellen White.

Theologians need to be fully converted and enlightened by the Holy Spirit, demonstrating an attitude of humility and a teachable spirit. They need to be united on the message and mission, not striving for originality or uniformity, but recognizing the presence of a healthy diversity in full harmony with the Bible and the Spirit of Prophecy.

Theologians ought to be very careful in the using and incorporating extra biblical sources and views in their writings and need to be fully aware of the threat to theological unity in the church through the use of extra biblical sources and views.

Finally, they need to have a sense of urgency in preparing people for Jesus' return. They must have the desire to be a part of the final call to present Christ's righteousness through a global mission proclamation of the loud cry message to hasten the return of Jesus, carefully paying attention to the light and counsels the Lord has given through His prophet.

4

Ellen White, Lifestyle, and Scripture Interpretation

Ellen White writes much on the study of the Bible. She carefully spells out the importance and use of proper principles of interpretation. However, it may come as a surprise to some, that, in her opinion, the use of a proper method of interpretation is not the most important factor in arriving at new divine truth.

She indicates that a crucial factor in discovering truth is a lifestyle dedicated to following fully the light that God has already given to the interpreter. The lifestyle determines whether one is able to receive the impulses of the Spirit in the study of Scripture. Lifestyle ultimately impacts the "How readest thou?" Lifestyle, therefore, may explain why interpreters, who apparently use even the same biblical principles to interpret the Bible, arrive at opposite views on the meaning of a text.

Why is lifestyle so significant? This question Ellen White discusses in the context of God's creative design of the human organism. Each human being is governed by laws which deal with the interrelationships regulating the operations between the body, mind and spirit. When God created Adam and Eve, they had a perfect lifestyle which contributed to the harmonious operation of all these faculties. The entrance of sin distorted this relationship, resulting in a sinful nature and lifestyle with all their detrimental results on body, mind and spirit.

Through the magnificent plan of redemption Christ has been working incessantly to restore in the fallen race the image of the Creator. Especially since the 19th century God has provided an abundance of

Originally published in the Journal of the Adventist Theological Society: Vol. 7: Iss. 2, 1996. Used with permission.

scientific knowledge about the laws of health and how they influence the proper function of the human body. This has led to a profound understanding of how the human organism might be restored to some degree to its original purpose—a harmonious operation of all human faculties. In this regard Ellen White provides much information on the best performance of body, mind, and spirit and their effect on the study of the Bible.

The Impact of Lifestyle on Spiritual Discernment

Ellen White presents the view that there exists an intimate relationship between the condition of the body and spiritual discernment. Said she, "Anything that lessens physical strength enfeebles the mind and makes it less capable of discriminating between right and wrong."[1] This means that "every wrong habit which injures the health of the body, reacts in effect upon the mind."[2] For the correct understanding of Bible truth we "need clear, energetic minds." Wrong lifestyle habits weaken the "intellectual powers."[3] By contrast, "right physical habits promote mental superiority. Intellectual power, physical strength, and longevity depend upon immutable laws."[4]

These convictions are based on her understanding of how God communicates His truth to humans. The part of the human body with which He interacts is the mind. Describing physiological processes, she states, "The brain nerves which communicate with the entire system are the only medium through which Heaven can communicate to man and affect his inmost life. Whatever disturbs the circulation of the electric currents in the nervous system lessens the strength of the vital powers, and the result is a deadening of the sensibilities of the mind"[5] This firmly establishes the principle that there is a strong relationship between health and spirituality, making it an absolute necessity to have a clear mind when engaged in the study of God's word.[6]

---

1   *Christ's Object Lessons*, 346.
2   *Healthful Living*, 195.
3   *Testimonies for the Church*, 2:66.
4   *Counsels on Diet and Foods*, 29.
5   *Testimonies for the Church*, 2:347.
6   *Testimonies for Ministers*, 114.

She says, "It is impossible for men and women, with all their sinful, health-destroying, brain- enervating habits, to discern sacred truth"[7]

In analyzing the factors which influence the mind, I discovered that what Ellen White calls "natural remedies," recommended for restoring the sick, also play an important role in assisting the brain to achieve top performance. These "remedies" are frequently listed as nutrition, water, exercise, air, sunlight, temperance, rest, and trust in divine power.

One of these remedies, temperance, regulates most of the others. In defining its scope, she said, "True temperance teaches us to dispense entirely with everything hurtful, and to use judiciously that which is healthful."[8] As will be shown below, the impact of these remedies on the brain and the subsequent effect on mind and spirituality is profound.

Physical Habits

Diet. No lifestyle dimension receives as much attention in her writings as that of nutrition. Ellen White points out that a variety of good food provides the necessary nourishment for the efficient operation of the brain. Delivering the nutrients to the mind involves converting food by digestion into basic elements which the blood transports throughout the whole system. The digestive as well as the circulatory systems are in charge of assuring that all brains cells receive adequate fuel for maximum performance. Anything that impairs the brain's function should be avoided. Unhealthful foods jeopardize these functions and "the mind is darkened,"[9] having in turn a negative affect on the outcome of one's study of the Scriptures.

The Quality of Food. Nutrition beneficial to the mind is found in a diet which strengthens the operation of the brain. The best foods, Ellen White says, are those that God originally provided for humanity: a vegetarian diet without the use of animal products. She writes: "In grains, fruits, vegetables, and nuts are to be found all the food

---

7   *Testimonies for the Church,* 3:162.
8   *Patriarchs and Prophets,* 562.
9   *Counsels on Diet and Foods,* 426.

elements that we need."[10] This is "the diet chosen for us by our Creator"[11] and contains "all the elements of nutrition."[12]

Nutrition that is detrimental to the brain should be avoided. This includes all flesh foods such as meat, poultry and fish. The exclusion is very important since their use does not provide "pure blood and clear minds."[13] Contrary to common opinion, flesh food produces "a poor quality of blood and flesh"[14] and "excites the animal propensities to increase activity and strengthens the animal passions."[15] Many fail to see that when this carnal nature is strengthened "the intellectual powers diminish proportionately."[16] This in turn "enfeebles the moral and spiritual nature"[17]

Other substances that jeopardize the mind are condiments and harmful spices. The use of "mustard, pepper, spices, pickles, and other things of a like character" irritates the stomach lining and eventually destroys its natural sensitiveness.[18] Spices also arouse the animal propensities and consequently weaken "the moral and intellectual powers"[19] and "becloud the reasoning faculties."[20]

Sugar is also a problem for the mind. It should be used sparingly.

Its free use is not good for the stomach because it "clogs the system," "hinders the working of the living machine,"[21] and causes "fermentation" which "clouds the brain."[22] In large quantities it is even

---

10   Ibid., 92.

11   *Ministry of Healing*, 296.

12   Practical Thoughts for Camp-Meetings," *Review and Herald,* May 8, 1883; *Education,* 204.

13   *Counsels and Diet and Foods,* 383.

14   *Testimonies for the Church,* 2:61.

15   Ibid., 63. She says: A meat diet "stimulates into intense activity the lustful propensities"; *Healthful Living,* 102.

16   *Healthful Living,* 101.

17   Ibid., 102. See also *Counsels on Diet and Foods,* 83.

18   *Ministry of Healing,* 325.

19   *Counsels on Health,* 114.

20   *Counsels on Diet and Foods,* 150.

21   *Testimonies for the Church,* 2:369.

22   *Counsels on Diet and Foods,* 331, 534, 535.

"more injurious than meat."[23] Rich, sweet desserts, therefore, should be avoided.[24]

Meals consisting largely of "soft foods, the soups and liquid foods" are not the best to produce "healthful muscles, sound digestive organs, or clear brains."[25] "Improper combinations of food" also create problems for the stomach. They produce "fermentation," causing the blood to be "contaminated and the brain confused."[26]

Eating Patterns. Ellen White gives much counsel against overeating, calling it "the sin of this age."[27] The seriousness of this pernicious habit is underscored by the fact that the Bible puts the sin of gluttony in the same category as drunkenness (Deut 21:20, 21).[28] Too much food overtaxes the stomach and seriously affects the mind. "The brain nerve energy is benumbed and almost paralyzed by overeating."[29] Overeating even leads to "forgetfulness and loss of memory."[30]

Eating irregularly or too frequently also affects the mind. "Irregular hours" for eating exhaust "the brain forces"[31] and "deprave the mind."[32] "The sin of intemperate eating, eating too frequently, too much, and of rich, unwholesome food, destroys the healthy action of the digestive organs, affects the brain, and perverts the judgment, preventing rational, calm, healthy thinking and acting."[33]

The impact of this type of lifestyle disqualifies a person for serious study of the Bible. "If our appetites are not under the control of a sanctified mind, if we are not temperate in all our eating and drinking," she says, "we shall not be in a state of mental and physical

---

23 *Testimonies for the Church,* 2:370.
24 She counseled that instead of spending money on unnecessary things like candy, gum, ice cream, and other knickknacks, these savings should be used for God's work (*Counsels on Diet and Foods,* 329).
25 *Fundamentals of Christian Education,* 226.
26 *Testimonies for the Church,* 7:257.
27 *Testimonies for the Church,* 4:454 (She warns that Seventh- day Adventists with all their profession of health reform eat too much. *Counsels on Diet and Foods,* 135).
28 *Testimonies for the Church,* 4:454.
29 *Testimonies for the Church,* 2:414.
30 *Counsels on Diet and Foods,* 138.
31 Word to Students," *Youth Instructor,* May 31, 1894, 174.
32 *Counsels on Diet and Foods,* 62.
33 *Testimonies for the Church,* 2:618, 619.

soundness to study the word with a purpose to learn what saith the Scripture."[34] She strongly appeals for the avoidance of all food "that has a tendency to irritate or excite the nerves. Excitement will be followed by depression; overindulgence will cloud the mind, and render thought difficult and confused. No man can become a successful workman in spiritual things until he observes strict temperance in his dietetic habits. God cannot let His Holy Spirit rest upon those who, while they know how they should eat for health, persist in a course that will enfeeble mind and body."[35]

"A disordered stomach is productive of a disordered, uncertain state of mind. A diseased stomach produces a diseased condition of the brain and often makes one obstinate in maintaining erroneous opinions."[36] It is not until people deny the gratification of the appetite and practice temperance in all things that they "may comprehend the truth in its beauty and clearness, and carry it out in their lives"[37]

Persons studying the Bible must keep the mind clear. Those who indulge perverted appetite in eating confuse the brain and will be unable "to bear the strain of digging deep" into the Scriptures.[38]

Drinking Habits. Drinking habits also affect the proper function of the brain. Water is the drink of choice. Extolling its benefits, Ellen White writes, "Pure water is one of heaven's choicest blessings. Its proper use promotes health. It is the beverage which God provided to quench the thirst of animals and man. Drunk freely, it helps to supply the necessities of the system, and assists nature to resist disease."[39] Water also assists in removing impurities form the blood [40] and is the "best liquid possible to cleanse the tissues."[41]

34 *Counsels on Diet and Foods,* 52.
35 Ibid., 55, 56.
36 *Testimonies for the Church,* 7:257.
37 *Testimonies for the Church,* 1:619.
38 *Testimonies to Ministers,* 114.
39 *Ministry of Healing,* 237.
40 *My Life Today,* 139.
41 "The Duty to Preserve Health," *Review and Herald,* July 29, 1884, 481.

She recommends the use of "pure soft water"[42] but expresses no objection to fruit juices provided they are "pure" and "free from fermentation."[43] Grape juice she describes as a "wholesome drink."[44]

Drinks to be avoided at all times are tea, coffee and alcoholic beverages. The difference between them is that tea, coffee and alcoholic drinks "are different degrees in the scale of artificial stimulants.[45] Describing their far-reaching impact on the body, White writes, "Through the use of stimulants, the whole system suffers. The nerves are unbalanced, the liver is morbid in its action, the quality and circulation of the blood are affected, and the skin becomes inactive and sallow."[46]

These beverages do not only affect the body but also the mind, distorting one's judgment. She explains: "The mind, too, is injured. The immediate influence of these stimulants is to excite the brain to undue activity, only to leave it weaker and less capable of exertion. The aftereffect is prostration, not only mental and physical, but moral. As a result, we see nervous men and women of unsound judgment and unbalanced mind."[47]

As with eating, wrong habits of drinking lead to "errors in thought and action."[48]Persons, therefore, whose appetite in drinking is perverted confuse their brain and mind. Consequently they will not be able to engage in deep Bible study.[49]

Physical Activity. Physical activities in the fresh air and sunshine are indispensable to the efficient operation of the mind and the correct interpretation of Scripture. Individuals frequently involved in the study of the Bible—such as students, scholars, theologians and minis-

---

42   *Counsels on Diet and Foods,* 419.

43   Ibid., 436.

44   Ibid., 436.

45   Ibid., 421.

46   Ibid., 422, 423.

47   Ibid., 423. A detrimental practice is the custom of drinking with meals. Using ice water during meals is especially harmful to the digestive system. Thirst can be quenched by drinking water a short time before or after the meal (Ibid., 420).

48   "Sanctification," *Review and Herald,* January 25, 1881, 50. Irregularity in drinking depraves the mind. (*Counsels on Diet and Foods,* 62).

49   *Testimonies to Ministers,* 114.

ters—are often given to a sedentary lifestyle. These occupations, Ellen White warns, are "the most dangerous, for they take men away from the open air and sunshine, and train one set of faculties, while other organs become weak from inaction."[50]

Exercise. The activities Ellen White recommends are those that strengthen the mind. For the greatest benefit these are to be done on a regular basis. She stresses the need for daily physical exercise.[51]

Although all physical activities have some benefit, not all forms of exercise are recommended. Exercise should be regulated and balanced. She points out that "the discipline of well regulated labor" is "essential to the securing of a strong and active mind and a noble character."[52] For maximum results one should balance activity of mind and body.[53] She recommends useful manual labor as the most beneficial exercise, not athletics or sports.[54]

The best place and time for exercise is out in the open air and during sunshine hours.[55] Gardening, which includes these components, is strongly recommended.[56] Walking, she considers as the best all-round form of exercise, because it uses "all the organs of the body," improving greatly the "circulation of the blood."[57] This form of exercise is readily available to all persons wherever they reside.

The benefits of exercise are extensive. It increases the circulation of the blood, improves the performance of muscles, veins [58] and lungs,[59] aids in "the work of digestion."[60] and improves the function

---

50 *Fundamentals of Christian Education,* 319.
51 *Gospel Workers* (1892), 173, "Daily outdoor exercise" she especially emphasized for persons who exercise little and spend much time indoors (*Testimonies for the Church,* 2:531, 533).
52 *Patriarchs and Prophets,* 601.
53 "Right Methods in Education," *Signs of the Times,* August 26, 1886, 513.
54 *Education,* 207-222.
55 "Right Methods in Education," *Signs of the Times,* August 26, 1886, 513.
56 *Gospel Workers* (1892), 174; Ibid., (1915), 240.
57 *Testimonies for the Church,* 3:78.
58 *Testimonies for the Church,* 2:529.
59 Ibid., 2:533.
60 Ibid., 2:530.

of the heart.[61] It also strengthens the liver and kidneys.[62] "Judicious exercise" will induce "the blood to the surface, and thus relieve the internal organs."[63] The more one exercises "the better will be the circulation of the blood"[64] which is indispensable for the efficient function and strengthening of the mind. As with all good things, one must take into consideration the principle of temperance. Much exercise without a proportional development of the mental powers forms an unbalanced lifestyle which is likewise detrimental to personal well-being.[65]

The Consequences of Inactivity. All who study the Bible seriously to discover truth must avoid inactivity at all costs, for it "is one of the greatest causes of debility of body and feebleness of mind."[66]

The detrimental effects of inactivity are compounded when persons live in unhealthful conditions. Residences which do not provide opportunity for sunshine in the rooms should be shunned.[67] All rooms should have plenty of light and a good circulation of fresh air.[68] Places with unhygienic premises should also be avoided because the inhaling of impure air pollutes the lungs, poisons the blood, and makes the whole system diseased.[69]

Persons who do not exercise in the fresh air are undermining their health. The absence of fresh air impedes the function of the skin. The pores of the skin through which the body breathes stay closed, Ellen White says, "making it impossible to throw off impurities." This leads to an overtaxation of "the liver, lungs, kidneys, etc." because these "internal organs are compelled to do the work of the skin."[70]

61 *Testimonies for the Church*, 3:490.
62 *Testimonies for the Church*, 2:533.
63 Ibid., 530.
64 Ibid., 525.
65 *Testimonies for the Church*, 3:157, 158.
66 *Testimonies for the Church*, 2:524.
67 *Ministry of Healing*, 274, 275; *Counsels on Health*, 57.
68 *Ministry of Healing*, 274.
69 *Healthful Living*, 172.
70 *Testimonies for the Church*, 2:524.

Prolonged inactivity finally leads to hypotrophy. Bowels become "enfeebled"[71] and muscles "decrease in size and strength," accompanied by a slowing down of the blood circulation.[72]

One important factor often neglected in obtaining an adequate supply of fresh air is shallow breathing. She remarked, "Stomach, liver, lungs, and brain are suffering for want of deep, full inspirations of air, which would electrify the blood and impart to it a bright, lively color, and which alone can keep it pure, and give tone and vigor to every part of the living machinery."[73] In order to have "good blood, we must breathe well."[74]

Thus "neglecting to exercise the entire body, or a portion of it, will bring on morbid conditions"[75] that will negatively impact the study of Scripture. A lifestyle with good habits of physical activity, therefore, is not optional, but a vital necessity for obtaining a strong, active mind which can clearly distinguish between truth and error.

Mental Habits

Mental activities such as reading and studying also have a profound influence on the mind. Ellen White recommends the reading of the Bible and books related to it as the best mental food for the development of the mind. The reading of story books, novels and frivolous exiting tales, however, have a detrimental effect on the mind. She explains that fictitious reading distorts the imagination and ultimately brings about a diseased imagination.[76] Consequently, it twists reality, leading to incorrect conclusions in the interpretation of the Bible.

Not only the type but also the amount of reading affects the mind. "Much reading" can weaken the moral and intellectual powers of the mind. "Strong minds," she says, "have been unbalanced and partially

---

71 *Testimonies for the Church,* 3:78.
72 Ibid., 76.
73 *Testimonies for the Church,* 2:67, 68.
74 *Healthful Living,* 171, 172.
75 *Testimonies for the Church,* 3:76.
76 "Search the Scriptures," *Review and Herald,* Nov. 28, 1878. See also Testimonies for the Church, 7:165, 203; *Counsels to Writers and Editors,* 134; *Messages to Young People,* 290.

benumbed, or paralyzed, by intemperance in reading."[77] "Intemperate habits of reading exert a pernicious influence upon the brain as surely as does intemperance in eating and drinking."[78] This habit is very detrimental to the brain. She cautions against "the gathering together of many books for study," because these often provide "a mass of knowledge that weakens the mind and makes it incapable of assimilating that which it has already received."[79] Consequently, "the mind becomes dyspeptic." Wisdom is needed to distinguish between these many authors and the Word of God.[80]

Persons in the habit of constantly studying the opinions of historians, theologians and other scholars are not much better off. She mentions that Christ "did not encourage any to attend the rabbinical schools of His day for the reason that their minds would be corrupted with the continually repeated, 'They say,' or, 'It has been said.'"[81] The sixth chapter of John, she says, has more to offer than "libraries filled with ponderous volumes of historical and theological lore."[82] "To a large degree theology, as studied and taught, is but a record of human speculation, serving only to darken 'counsel by words without knowledge' Job 38:2."[83] The "laborious study of the opinions of men" tends to enfeeble rather than strengthen a person.[84] She said, "A study of the many different authors confuses and wearies the mind, and has a detrimental influence upon the religious life."[85]

The mental faculties are also weakened by an overload of studies. "Many," she said, "are crowding too many studies into a limited period of time. They are overworking their mental powers; and as a consequence they see many things in a perverted light... They become unbalanced in mind."[86]

---

77 *Testimonies for the Church,* 2:410.
78 *Fundamentals of Christian Education,* 164.
79 *Testimonies for the Church,* 7:205.
80 Ibid., 7:205. She exhorts, "Let us close the door to so much reading." See also *Fundamentals of Christian Education,* 446, 447.
81 *Testimonies for the Church,* 8:31.
82 *Counsels to Parents, Teachers, and Students,* 379.
83 Ibid., 380.
84 Ibid., 379.
85 *Fundamentals of Christian Education,* 446.
86 Ibid., 350.

Ellen White perceives that in the area of mental habits, a person needs to put the Bible in the center of all his/her reading and study. This will strengthen the mind and avoid any distortion of the imagination to prevent unsound conclusions in the interpretation of the Bible.

Pleasure Habits. Ellen White considers the indulgence of the passions very damaging. It "beclouds the mind, lessens physical strength, and weakens moral power." As a result the "thoughts are not clear." The subjection of animal passions to the higher spiritual nature is absolutely vital for having correct reasoning powers. Says Ellen White, "the control of all the passions will preserve the intellect and give mental and moral vigor, enabling men to bring all their propensities under the control of the higher powers and to discern between right and wrong, the sacred and the common."[87]

One passion she specifically identified is excessive sexual activity within marriage. This may cause "paralysis of nerve and brain"[88] "Sensual indulgence weakens the mind and debases the soul. The moral and intellectual powers are benumbed and paralyzed by the gratification of the animal propensities."[89] Another passion she warns against is the destructive effects of self-pollution, also termed self-abuse (masturbation).[90]

Frivolous, worldly pleasure parties[91] and exciting amusements have an unfavorable influence on physical strength and mental powers. Explaining the effects of these amusements, Ellen White writes, "The mind is not kept in a calm, healthful state for thought, but is, much of the time, under an excitement; in short, is intoxicated with the amusements it craves, which renders it incapable of close application, reflection, and study."[92]

Although Ellen White condemns the above pleasure habits, she recognizes that the human body and brain need diversion and rest so they can be restored. Overworking beclouds the intellect and decrea-

---

87 *Testimonies for the Church,* 3:491.
88 *Testimonies for the Church,* 2:477.
89 *Patriarchs and Prophets,* 458.
90 *Testimonies for the Church,* 2:481.
91 *Testimonies for the Church,* 8:66.
92 "The Life of Christ, No. 9," *Youth Instructor,* Sept. 1873, 69.

ses spirituality.[93] She says, "If the brain were given proper periods of rest, the thoughts would be clear and shar"[94] "Proper periods of sleep and rest" are essential to health of body and mind.[95] Irregular hours for sleeping impair the brain.[96]

However instead of being involved in amusement that is "sought for the sake of pleasure, and is often carried to excess" she recommends that Christians should spend their leisure time in "recreation" which "when true to its name, recreation, tends to strengthen and build u Calling us aside from our ordinary cares and occupations, it affords refreshment for mind and body."[97] This form of activity prepares the mind for a renewed invigorating study of the Scriptures.

Spiritual Habits

The spiritual habits of persons in search of truth are the key to a total Christ-like lifestyle. Those imitating such a lifestyle realize that in themselves they are incapable of living the life which would place them in a position to receive new light on the Scriptures. They know that they must have the grace of God in order to be fully obedient to the laws of life. "Men will never be truly temperate," she says, "until the grace of Christ is an abiding principle in the heart," and "their hearts are transformed by the grace of God."[98] It is the outworking of this grace which brings the desired results about. "The minds of all who are renewed by grace will be an open medium, continually receiving light, grace, and truth from above, and transmitting the same to others."[99]

A Relationship with Christ. Persons with a vital connection with Christ will receive further light. Ellen White says, "new light will ever be revealed on the word of God to him who is in living connection

---

93 *Testimonies for the Church,* 1:488; *Testimonies for the Church,* 2:71.
94 *Testimonies for the Church,* 7:256.
95 Ibid., 247.
96 "Word to Students," *Youth Instructor,* May 31, 1894, 174.
97 *Education,* 207. The recreation she especially recommends takes place in the countryside where one can enjoy the beauty of nature. Family outings where parents and children join each other in healthy picnics and exercise in the open air will bring new life so all can face life's duties with new courage (*Adventist Home,* 498-520).
98 *Counsels on Diet and Foods,* 35.
99 *Testimonies for the Church,* 2:488.

with the Sun of Righteousness."[100] The results are far- reaching. When the believer has such a relationship with Christ so that it can be said he/she, eats His flesh and drinks His blood, as it were, "the old truths will be presented, but they will be seen in a new light. There will be a new perception of truth, a clearness and a power that all will discern."[101] As long as persons are growing in grace "they will be constantly obtaining a clearer understanding of His word. They will discern new light and beauty in its sacred truths."[102]

Obeying the Light Already Revealed. Obedience to the light God has already given determines whether the interpreter will receive further light. Ellen White points out that "it is when we walk in the light that shines upon us, obeying the truth that is open to our understanding, that we receive greater light."[103] Those only who faithfully accept and appreciate the light God has given us, and who take a high, noble stand in self-denial and self- sacrifice, will be channels of light to the world."[104] Those who do not follow the light as fast as the providence of God reveals it will be "in darkness."[105]

Depending on God. A lifestyle of continued dependence upon God is more significant than all education and scholarshi Ellen White explains: "It is sometimes the case that men of intellectual ability, improved by education and culture, fail to comprehend certain passages of Scripture, while others who are uneducated, whose understanding seems weak and whose minds are undisciplined, will grasp the meaning, finding strength and comfort in that which the former declare to be mysterious or pass by as unimportant."

How is this possible? What makes the difference? She replies: "It has been explained to me that the latter class do not rely upon their own understanding. They go to the Source of light, the One who has inspired the Scriptures. and with humility of heart ask God for wisdom, and they receive it."[106]

100 *Counsels to Writers and Editors,* 35.
101 *Christ's Object Lessons,* 130, 131.
102 *Testimonies for the Church,* 5:706.
103 *My Life Today,* 310.
104 *Testimonies for the Church,* 5:534.
105 *Testimonies for the Church,* 2:67.
106 *Testimonies for the Church,* 5:704.

Respect and Reverence for the Bible. The respectful treatment of the Scriptures is another important factor determining whether the mind will be enlightened during the interpreter's study. "When the word of God is opened without reverence and without prayer; when the thoughts and affections are not fixed upon God or in harmony with His will, the mind is clouded with doubt; and in the very study of the Bible, skepticism strengthens. The enemy takes control of the thoughts, and he suggests interpretations that are not correct."[107]

Conclusion

From this investigation we have observed that the lifestyle has a very significant impact on the brain/mind and the outcome of the study of Scripture. It is clear that differences in lifestyle can be a determining factor in why interpreters of the Bible come to opposite conclusions on the meaning of Bible passages even when using the same principles of interpretation.

There are, however, so many lifestyle factors which may influence Bible interpretation—such as eating, drinking, level of physical activity, type of reading and amusements, a personal relationship to Christ, obedience to the divine light, an attitude of total dependence upon God and a reverence for the Bible—that it is impossible to draw conclusions regarding the validity of the interpretation simply on the basis of a given exegesis of the text. The difficulty of obtaining accurate information on all those factors is a major reason why Ellen White strongly encourages persons to bring their lives into full harmony with God's moral and health laws, imitate the life of Christ and focus their study on the Scriptures instead of Bible commentaries.

Her concern is for God's people to grow unitedly in the understanding of the truth as it in Jesus. She strongly encourages God's remnant to purify their minds so that their blurred vision may clear u This general lack of clear perception explains why she calls the remnant church Laodicea, a community with a distorted vision and a misconception of their true condition. They think they are rich, but really

---

107 Ibid., 704, 705.

their poverty is plainly visible because they are naked and have nothing to give (Rev. 3:14-19).

True, there are exceptions, but overall the picture is one of poverty. If they listen to the Heavenly Merchant, believe, and do what He tells them, their situation will improve. It is only when His people realize they are nothing in themselves and that their righteous deeds and academic works are like filthy rags, that there is any hope. When the truth is perceived as it is in Jesus, when the Lamb of God is lifted up in all His glory, then the Savior will disclose Himself with His present truth message.

It is, therefore, of crucial importance for His people to remove the last vestiges of a worldly and unhealthy lifestyle so that the love and righteousness of Christ can shine through their dedicated, transparent lives. Only then will the world see the unity for which Christ prayed—a unity in faith, doctrine, and lifestyle, powerfully proclaiming the good news of His imminent return.

Your opinion counts! if you bought this book on Amazon, please share your rating and honest review of this book. Your feedback will be invaluable in guiding others in their decision to purchase this powerful work.

And that's not all. Want to spread this blessing even further? Here's how:

a. Share the wisdom: Purchase additional copies of this book and share them with your loved ones, friends, colleagues and community. Make this source of inspiration reach every corner where it can make a difference.

b. Support the mission: Make a tax-free donation on the saetadesalvacion.org website to support the distribution of this book in Spanish-speaking countries. A committed team is ready to take this material to churches and communities, your contribution will make this noble purpose possible!

Your participation makes a difference!

Together, we can extend the transformational impact of this work.

Join our community! Subscribe to our mailing list and find out more about this work and other publications that will inspire you. Visit our website **arrowofsalvation.org** and begin your journey towards spiritual transformation and growth.

Don't miss this opportunity to explore a world of knowledge and wisdom! Your next step towards a fuller and more meaningful life awaits you on our website.

Scan the code to access our website **arrowofsalvation.org**

"Beloved, I pray that you may prosper in all things,
and be in health, just as your soul prospers."

3 John 1:2

May the Lord richly bless you, your friends and brothers of Arrow of Salvation.

Made in the USA
Middletown, DE
05 July 2024

56902356R00064